Understanding and Implementing Reading First Initiatives

THE CHANGING ROLE OF ADMINISTRATORS

Carrice Cummins, Editor
Louisiana Tech University
Ruston, Louisiana, USA

INTERNATIONAL
Reading Association
800 BARKSDALE ROAD, PO BOX 8139
NEWARK, DE 19714-8139, USA
www.reading.org

KH

The International Reading Association attempts, through its publications, to provide a forum for a wide spectrum of opinions on reading. This policy permits divergent viewpoints without implying the endorsement of the Association.

Director of Publications   Dan Mangan
Editorial Director, Books and Special Projects   Teresa Curto
Managing Editor, Books   Shannon T. Fortner
Acquisitions and Developmental Editor   Corinne M. Mooney
Associate Editor   Charlene M. Nichols
Associate Editor   Elizabeth C. Hunt
Production Editor   Amy Messick
Books and Inventory Assistant   Rebecca A. Zell
Permissions Editor   Janet S. Parrack
Assistant Permissions Editor   Tyanna L. Collins
Production Department Manager   Iona Muscella
Supervisor, Electronic Publishing   Anette Schütz
Senior Electronic Publishing Specialist   R. Lynn Harrison
Electronic Publishing Specialist   Lisa M. Kochel
Proofreader   Stacey Lynn Sharp

Project Editor   Charlene M. Nichols

Art   Cover Design, Linda Steere; Cover Photos (from left): © Getty Images, Inc., © Getty Images, Inc., © comstock.com; Interior Photos (from left): © Getty Images, Inc., © comstock.com, © comstock.com, © Getty Images, Inc.; Interior Illustrations (pp. 24, 110), Linda Steere

Web addresses in this book were correct as of the publication date but may have become inactive or otherwise modified since that time. If you notice a deactivated or changed Web address, please e-mail books@reading.org with the words "Website Update" in the subject line. In your message, specify the Web link, the book title, and the page number on which the link appears.

Library of Congress Cataloging-in-Publication Data

Understanding and implementing Reading First initiatives : the changing role of administrators / Carrice Cummins, editor.
    p. cm.
  Includes bibliographical references and index.
  ISBN 0-87207-593-1
  1. Reading--United States. 2. School management and organization--United States. 3. Educational leadership--United States. 4. Literacy programs--United States. 5. Educational planning--United States. I. Cummins, Carrice, 1955-

LB1050.2.U53 2006
379.24--dc22

2005028342

Second Printing, April 2006

10/19/06

To administrators everywhere who work hard
to support teachers and students
in their literacy development.

CONTENTS

FOREWORD

Effective school reform requires knowledgeable and capable leadership. Yet, in the haste to develop and implement literacy programs that meet current demands for educational reform in the United States, the role of administrators is often neglected. Carrice Cummins has assembled an outstanding group of scholars to produce an excellent resource for today's administrators of literacy programs. Literacy professionals will embrace this book as the missing link in their overall effort for program improvement.

Today's school administrators face demands that have been characterized as unprecedented in complexity and challenge. This is particularly true in literacy education. Administrators must constantly juggle the sometimes conflicting demands of instruction, management, and policy. At the same time, they must reconcile local school demands with those that are imposed by others, whether they be at the district, state, and/or national level. Instructional leaders are challenged to ensure that their schools "measure up," which is often interpreted to mean better scores on reading assessments.

Ironically, administrators often come to their positions with limited backgrounds in literacy education. Some may have little or no classroom teaching experience at the levels most affected by recent mandates. Others may be challenged by new terminology and academic requirements. Obviously, administrators do not work alone. They work with specialists and classroom teachers to meet reform requirements. Nevertheless, as instructional leaders, they should possess a sufficient knowledge base to be informed guides, critical observers, and helpful participants in reform activities. In short, they should be able to ask good questions of those with whom they work and have delegated responsibility. Understandably, they need reliable, on-the-job resources in order to do this.

This edited collection provides an invaluable resource in support of administrators' knowledge and practice. The contributors write in a highly readable and accessible style. At the same time, they take care to provide content that is accurate and substantive. One can imagine administrators entering this book at any point and finding the information needed to answer pressing questions and strengthen their knowledge base. I highly recommend *Understanding and Implementing Reading First Initiatives: The Changing Role of Administrators*.

Dorothy S. Strickland
Samuel DeWitt Proctor Professor of Education
Rutgers, The State University of New Jersey

ACKNOWLEDGMENTS

First and foremost, I thank all of the contributors of this book. I never dreamed that I would have the privilege of working with such an astute group of professionals. The knowledge, dedication, and passion for the field of literacy they possess collectively is astounding. Thanks to each of you for helping me (and putting up with me) on my maiden voyage as an editor—it has been a remarkable adventure.

I would also like to thank the many administrators throughout Louisiana and beyond who were instrumental in supporting and guiding me during my tenure as a district-level administrator. Appreciation is especially extended to the district- and school-level administrators, past and present, of the Richland Parish School Board, Rayville, Louisiana. All of these individuals taught me a lot about teaching and learning and the power of working together.

Special thanks are extended to

- Dr. Arlon Adams and Billy Joe Lyles, for "convincing" me that I had a role to play in administration.
- Bonnie Adams, for keeping me on my toes and reminding me to always look at the "whole picture" before making decisions.
- Keith Pruitt, for modeling the importance of listening to and caring about the people you work with and for always believing in me.
- My editor, Charlene Nichols, for her patience, precise attention to details, and for her ability to sense what I was trying to say and then helping me match language to my intentions.

And of course I would be remiss if I failed to thank those closest to me: my husband, Bill; my children, Mason and Christi; and my grandchildren, Kelcey and Brason. Their constant understanding about Mom/Mema "being busy" is deeply appreciated.

CONTRIBUTORS

Sherry L. Alleman
Title I Director/Reading Specialist
Milford Public Schools
Milford, Massachusetts, USA

Richard L. Allington
Professor of Education
University of Tennessee
Knoxville, Tennessee, USA

Rita M. Bean
Professor of Education
University of Pittsburgh
Pittsburgh, Pennsylvania, USA

Cathy Collins Block
Professor of Education
Texas Christian University
Fort Worth, Texas, USA

Kathryn E. Carroll
Kindergarten Teacher
Pittsburgh Public Schools
Pittsburgh, Pennsylvania, USA

Martha A. Colwell
Principal
Woodland Elementary School
Milford, Massachusetts, USA

Carrice Cummins
Associate Professor of Education
Louisiana Tech University
Ruston, Louisiana, USA

Billie J. Enz
Associate Division Director,
    Division of Curriculum
    & Instruction
Arizona State University
Tempe, Arizona, USA

James Flood
Distinguished Professor
    of Language and Literacy
San Diego State University
San Diego, California, USA

Sharon Flood
Lecturer in Education
San Diego State University
San Diego, California, USA

Linda B. Gambrell
Professor of Education
Clemson University
Clemson, South Carolina, USA

Diane Lapp
Distinguished Professor
of Language and Literacy
San Diego State University
San Diego, California, USA

Jacquelynn A. Malloy
Doctoral Student
Eugene T. Moore School of
Education, Clemson University
Clemson, South Carolina, USA

Heather Morgan
Fifth-Grade Teacher
Greenwich Elementary School
Stewartsville, New Jersey, USA

Lesley Mandel Morrow
Professor of Literacy
Rutgers, The State University
of New Jersey
New Brunswick, New Jersey, USA

Timothy V. Rasinski
Professor of Literacy Education
Kent State University
Kent, Ohio, USA

Timothy Shanahan
Professor of Urban Education
University of Illinois at Chicago
Chicago, Illinois, USA

Margaret Taylor Stewart
Associate Professor, Coordinator
of Elementary Education and
Director of Student Licensure
Lees-McRae College
Banner Elk, North Carolina, USA

Gwendolyn Smith Williams
Assistant Professor
Bowie State University
Bowie, Maryland, USA

Sarah Nelson Womble
Leadership Development
Associate
International Reading Association
Sherwood, Arkansas, USA

INTRODUCTION

Carrice Cummins

> "A good school for me is a place in which everyone
> is teaching and everyone is learning, simultaneously,
> under the same roof. Students are teaching and
> learning; principals are teaching and learning;
> teachers are teaching and learning."
>
> Barth, 1990, p. 512

The current education agenda arising from implementation of the No Child Left Behind (NCLB) Act of 2001 (2002); Reading First; and other local, state, and federal mandates in the United States require that administrators and teachers work together to improve reading achievement for all students. Today more than ever educators face escalating demands including understanding and implementing legislative mandates, providing high-quality instruction, addressing technology and other resource needs with a limited budget, coping with increasing populations of non–English-speaking students, and dealing with an overwhelming array of outside influences. Yet schools are expected to meet the literacy needs of all students. Even to attempt to accomplish this awesome task, administrators must be excellent managers and also be attuned to current literacy issues. Education is not a one-sided phenomenon—teachers teaching or students learning. Rather, it is a continuous cycle of all stakeholders—teachers, students, *and* administrators—teaching and learning. Administrators must learn *and* teach alongside teachers and students. The current need for leaders in literacy instruction at both the school and district levels has never been greater.

Traditionally, administrators at the school and district levels have been hired for their abilities to be good managers. Today, however, administrators require two types of expertise to make a serious impact on literacy in schools: (1) expertise in leading the *change process* and (2) expertise in the *content* of literacy (Fullan, 2001). Both are essential to improving schools, but the increased emphasis nationwide on literacy development recognizes the need for today's administrators to be strong instructional leaders who are knowledgeable not only in the law governing current issues related to literacy but also in strategies and practices that address these issues within the classroom setting. This paradigm shift has put many administrators in an awkward position because some of them may be expert change agents but novice literacy educators, or vice versa. Just as teachers scaffold instruction for their students, administrators' transitions from managers to literacy instructional leaders also must be scaffolded. This text can help serve as the initial knowledge base for building administrators' background knowledge in areas deemed essential to appropriate literacy instruction, and it can also help open the door for more detailed investigations into these areas as administrators become ready to do so.

The Need for Literacy Leadership

One catalyst affecting the need for leaders in literacy instruction is the implementation of legislative mandates outlined in NCLB. NCLB states that its overall purpose is "to ensure that all children have a fair, equal, and significant opportunity to obtain a high-quality education and reach, at a minimum, proficiency on challenging state standards and assessments" (115 Stat. 1425, 2002, ¶1). Key purposes interwoven within this statement include closing the achievement gap between high- and low-performing students, administering annual academic assessments to measure the achievement of all students, providing reading instruction aligned with scientifically based reading research, and demonstrating adequate yearly progress for all students.

These purposes are further developed in the law under Part B—Student Reading Skills Improvement Grants, Subpart 1—otherwise known as Reading First. Reading First proposes to provide assistance to state and local educational agencies in establishing sound reading programs for K–3 students, specifically in districts and schools with a high percentage of students reading below grade level and/or living in poverty. The law does not specifically define the term *reading program* nor does it mandate the use of any one program; however, it does specify that programs be designed to meet the needs of students based on scientifically based reading research, and the instruction must focus on the five essential components of reading instruction named in NCLB: (1) phonemic awareness, (2) phonics, (3) vocabulary, (4) fluency, and (5) comprehension. Although Reading First mandates only directly affect districts and schools receiving funds through this subpart of NCLB, it should be noted that many states are beginning to require that all K–3 programs align with provisions in their Reading First applications.

Because NCLB is law, educational administrators in states accepting Reading First funds find themselves conducting the work of teaching and learning within its constraints. This work often falls under the domain of administrators who possess exemplary administrative skills but may have limited backgrounds in early literacy and reading instruction. However, accomplishing the goals of NCLB mandates requires that administrators rely on their abilities both as change agents and as instructional leaders.

Before administrators can make instructional decisions for their districts or schools and provide support for teachers, they must have, at the minimum, a basic understanding of the components required for successful reading instruction. In 2000, the National Reading Panel (NRP) summarized a body of quantitative research on reading instruction focused on the critical years of kindergarten through grade 3 in *Report of the National Reading Panel. Teaching Children to Read: An Evidence-Based Assessment of the Scientific Research Literature on Reading and Its Implications for Reading Instruction* (National Institute of Child Health and Human Development). The research review uncovered numerous topics important to the teaching of reading, and ultimately, the panel identified some basic elements necessary for effective reading instruction. Based on the work of the NRP, Congress passed NCLB, which then named five components essential to effective reading instruction: (1) phonemic awareness, (2) phonics, (3) vocabulary, (4) fluency, and (5) comprehension. These elements are crucial to the development of reading; however, limiting the focus of reading instruction to these five components might eliminate teaching emphasis on other important areas of literacy development, such as oral language, writing, and motivation. Oral language development is central to reading success; writing is best taught when directly connected to reading; and if students are not motivated to read, then they probably will not. As important as each of these instructional components are, none can stand alone and be taught in isolation; that is, each component represents an interlocking piece of the complex process of reading.

The Purpose and Audience of This Volume

Individual studies, publications, or both are available for each of the previously mentioned reading instruction components; however, locating and reading this multitude of sources is time-consuming. In addition, many of these resources are often written from a theoretical perspective, and many administrators, especially those with a limited background in reading, are frustrated with the complexity of the explanations. This volume provides a general snapshot of each of the five essential elements outlined in Reading First as well as additional components relevant to reading instruction (i.e., oral language, writing, motivation). Each component is addressed in an accessible and reader-friendly format designed to provide general background information and suggestions for classroom implementation.

The goal of this volume is to offer basic knowledge in the crucial areas of reading instruction to school- and district-level administrators so they can support teachers in their efforts to help all students grow as readers and writers. In addition, this volume offers strategies that administrators can use to support teachers in their literacy instruction and to serve as a springboard for further and more intense study of specific areas of literacy need within their schools and districts.

Although written with the administrator in mind, this resource also can and should be used by teachers, teacher educators, staff developers, policymakers, and others interested in supporting literacy in U.S. schools.

Overview

This volume consists of 12 chapters: Three chapters focus on issues related to instructional leadership, and the remaining nine chapters each explore a different element of literacy development—intermingling background information, theory, and practical application. Chapter 1 provides background information regarding the role of administrators as leaders in literacy instruction. To bring about change targeted at increased student achievement in the area of reading, administrators must understand the teaching and learning required in a sound literacy program. Chapters 2–6 each focus on a different essential element of reading instruction as identified in NCLB: phonemic awareness, phonics, vocabulary, fluency, and comprehension. Chapters 7 and 8 address two additional elements of reading instruction—oral language development and writing, respectively—that directly influence or extend the components explained in previous chapters. Chapter 9 discusses the role of motivation in helping students attend to reading instruction, an area noted as important by both the NRP and NCLB. Students who are not motivated to read will most likely not be interested in learning to read; therefore, motivation is of crucial importance. Regardless of the reading instruction provided, schools and districts may still have readers who need extra assistance. Chapter 10 provides additional information and strategies for working with these struggling readers. Chapter 11 focuses on literacy coaches—an important component of Reading First— and ways that they can support administrators and teachers in providing quality reading instruction for all children. The last chapter features a journey of change made by a present school-level administrator and literacy coach as they worked with teachers and students in developing a sound literacy program.

Reading This Volume

Each chapter of this book may be read in isolation, as needed; however, the full synergy occurs when the chapters are viewed as interlocking pieces of reading instruction that together form a cohesive whole. Initially, administrators are encouraged to read the book in its entirety to deepen their base knowledge of early reading instruction and then pull sections, strategies, or both, as needed, when working with teachers to meet the literacy needs of students. The strategies provided within each chapter are written in such a way that they can easily be "lifted" and shared with teachers.

Even though the content of this book is written more directly for administrators working with teachers and students in grades K–3 in Reading First schools, the information is valuable for all administrators and teachers working with students in these grades. In addition, many of the strategies—especially in the areas of vocabulary, fluency, comprehension, writing, oral language, motivation, and working with struggling readers—can be modified for use with students in higher grade levels.

It has long been debated whether reading is a science or an art. Judy Cohen, a colleague from the University of Chicago, once commented that "reading is a science taught by an artist" (personal communication, April 15, 2004). Administrators work with teachers every day; therefore, it is crucial that they understand the "science" involved in reading as well as have a command of basic strategies that will allow them to help teachers provide the appropriate brush strokes necessary for painting a complete reading picture.

Teachers must attend to all students in their care. Knowledgeable and caring teachers are the key to implementing instruction in ways that meet the needs of all students while also instilling a love for reading; however, teachers are not in this work alone. Administrators, at all levels, also must know when and with what tools to assist teachers in this endeavor because the need for literacy leadership has never been greater than it is today. When administrators, teachers, and students learn and teach together, amazing things happen.

Editor's Note: As a past administrator, I worked with many other administrators, each with his or her own special area of expertise. I called on many of these individuals for help in dealing with the managerial tasks, and many of them called on me for issues concerning literacy. I hope this book will provide some suggestions that will seem workable for your particular learning situation and may spark ideas that will send you to other resources that will be helpful to you.

REFERENCES

Barth, R.S. (1990). A personal vision of a good school. *Phi Delta Kappan, 71*(7), 512–516.

Fullan, M. (2001). *The new meaning of educational change* (3rd ed.). New York: Teachers College Press.

National Institute of Child Health and Human Development. (2000). *Report of the National Reading Panel. Teaching children to read: An evidence-based assessment of the scientific research literature on reading and its implications for reading instruction* (NIH Publication No. 00-4769). Washington, DC: U.S. Government Printing Office.

No Child Left Behind Act of 2001, Pub. L. No. 107-110, 115 Stat. 1425 (2002). Retrieved October 1, 2005, from http://edworkforce.house.gov/issues/107th/education/nclb/nclb.htm

CHAPTER 1

The Leadership Role of Administrators in the Era of No Child Left Behind

Sarah Nelson Womble

WHILE MRS. MCCOLLUM is working with a group of her third-grade students, the principal, Mrs. Quillen, visits the classroom to observe. The students take turns reading from a leveled text. Mrs. Quillen notices that the students are fidgety and not engaged in the lesson. One of the students speaks up and says, "Mrs. McCollum, this is boring, and I am tired of reading the same thing over and over." Mrs. McCollum, obviously uncomfortable, replies, "Josh, I am sorry you are bored." Mrs. Quillen quietly leaves the room.

After the students leave for the day, Mrs. Quillen returns to discuss the lesson with Mrs. McCollum. She begins by asking Mrs. McCollum about her instructional goals for the lesson. Mrs. McCollum replies that she was working on a fluency lesson with the students because a recent assessment indicated a need for additional instruction. Mrs. Quillen praises her for using assessment data to inform instruction in this area. She then asks for Mrs. McCollum's opinion regarding the effectiveness of the repeated reading strategy she used with the students. Mrs. McCollum quickly replies that she knows the students were bored with the lesson, and it was difficult keeping them engaged. Then, Mrs. Quillen shares an article on repeated reading she had brought with her. The article suggests using Readers Theatre to incorporate repeated reading in an interesting and meaningful way so students have a real purpose for the repeated readings—that is, preparing to perform the selection for an *audience*. The two educators discuss how Mrs. McCollum might use the information and adapt it to her fluency lesson for the next day.

I n the vignette, the school principal exemplifies her role as an instructional literacy leader: Mrs. Quillen is able to identify the instructional goal being addressed and take steps to support the teacher in modifying her instruction to be more effective. In response to the No Child Left Behind Act of 2001 (NCLB; 2002) and its emphasis on school accountability for student achievement, current trends in school leadership reflect the view of administrators as instructional leaders.

Under NCLB, state and local school systems are required to close the achievement gap with accountability, flexibility, and choice so no student lacks the support needed for success. As previously mentioned, Reading First, a subpart of NCLB, is a competitive grant program created to help states and school districts set up "scientific research based" reading programs for students in kindergarten through third grade (with priority given to high-poverty areas). Some of the purposes of this initiative include the following:

- establishing reading programs;
- providing professional development and other support;
- selecting or administering screening, diagnostic, and classroom-based instructional reading assessments;
- selecting or developing effective instructional materials; and
- strengthening coordination among schools, early literacy programs, and family literacy programs.

For state and local school systems to meet the requirements of NCLB and Reading First, administrators working in schools that include kindergarten through third grade must take on the role of instructional leader. It is important to note that even though the phrase *instructional leader* most often refers to building-level administrators (i.e., principals), district-level administrators working with principals and teachers also must be knowledgeable in matters of instruction.

The Changing Roles of Administrators

The role of building-level administrators has changed several times over the past 25 years. Many educators are probably familiar with the saying, "An experienced administrator is one who has been hit by the pendulum more than once," which seems particularly appropriate at this time. In regard to the role of administrators, the pendulum has swung from instructional leader in the 1980s to school-based manager and facilitator in the early 1990s and back to instructional leader in the 21st century.

Although the term *instructional leader* may be familiar to educators, the meaning behind the term has changed drastically over time. In the 1980s, the major responsibilities of instructional leaders included monitoring the curriculum, reviewing lesson plans, and evaluating teachers. In the era of NCLB, the responsibilities have increased significantly thus placing even greater demands on administrators. Today, administrators need to be skilled in and more directly involved in the implementation of instructional practices. Therefore, they must be more knowledgeable about assessment and the use of data for making instructional decisions. They need to be knowledgeable about literacy content as well as the most effective ways to implement that content in the classroom. They also need to be aware of appropriate professional development to meet the specific needs of the students in their school and district. Finally, they need to be involved in the development of the curriculum. Regardless of the overarching framework for this role, however, the research evidence is clear: Administrators play a critical leadership role that enables the school and district to provide an effective reading program for its students.

Perhaps the most daunting reality of this new role of instructional leader is the responsibility placed on schools and school leadership by NCLB to ensure that every child is a reader by the end of third grade. This presents not only a challenge to building-level administrators but also a problem that has to be solved. Former U.S. President John F. Kennedy once commented that on the night before his inauguration former U.S. President Eisenhower told him, "You'll find no easy problems ever come to the President of the United States. If they are easy, somebody else has solved them." Administrators can certainly identify with this statement. Assuring that every child is a reader by third grade is neither an easy problem to solve nor a problem someone else has already solved. The managerial tasks required of building-level administrators have not diminished and are obviously still important. Administrators typically deal with issues concerning the "Four Bs"—budgets, buses, buildings, and behavior—on a daily basis. Effective administrators also recognize the importance of eliciting parental involvement and spending time communicating with parents. Today's administrators are not managers *or* instructional leaders—they must be both.

Deal and Peterson (1994) suggest that educators need to think of new ways to combine leading and managing. The concept of yin and yang used by ancient Chinese philosophers can be used to illustrate the importance of balancing leadership and management. This concept indicates that through the combination of two opposites a unified whole is created. Neither yin nor yang can exist without the other. Because literacy learning is currently at the forefront of discussions about education, administrators must take on the expanded role of instructional leaders in literacy while continuing to perform managerial duties.

The Instructional Leader in Today's School

As previously mentioned, instructional leadership is required to meet the demands facing administrators, their districts, their schools, and their teachers in today's current education climate. McEwan (2002) offers the following seven steps to effective instructional leadership as guidance to administrators as they move into this new role of leadership:

- Establish, implement, and achieve academic standards.
- Be an instructional resource for staff.
- Create a learning-oriented school culture and climate.
- Communicate the school's vision and mission to staff and students.
- Set high expectations for the staff and yourself.
- Develop teacher leaders.
- Develop and maintain positive relationships with students, staff, and parents. (p. 15)

Effective administrators are knowledgeable of the underlying issues that support each of the steps of effective leadership. For example, to develop teacher leaders, a climate that supports collaborative professional development first must be established. Effective leaders also must recognize the role each step plays in improving the school's efforts to strengthen reading instruction, and they must be able to implement each step—not as isolated entities but as a cohesive whole working together to make an impact on student learning and achievement.

In addition, in a study conducted by Blasé and Blasé (2000), when teachers were asked to describe behaviors of administrators who had made an impact on student learning, two major themes were identified: (1) talking to teachers about instructional issues and (2) promoting their professional growth. Teachers also understood that learning was directly influenced when principals talked to teachers inside and outside of instructional conferences, gave praise for effective teaching, made suggestions or gave advice for improvement of instruction, and provided opportunities for professional development (Blasé & Blasé, 2000).

In the remainder of the chapter, I combine the findings from McEwan and Blasé and Blasé and discuss the emergent concepts.

Establishing, Implementing, and Achieving Academic Standards

Establishing, implementing, and achieving academic standards are essential steps in improving student academic growth. Many states have identified required standards, making implementation of the standards a priority at both the district and school levels. A fundamental piece of this implementation involves assessment. Because accountability through assessment is such an important part of NCLB, it is essential that administrators understand how assessment can help inform instruction. In addition, administrators must be aware that assessment has certain limitations. Performance on one assessment should not be the only factor taken into consideration when making decisions about individual students. Students have a right to reading assessment that identifies their strengths as well as their needs and involves them in making decisions about their own learning (International Reading Association [IRA], 2000). What is taught and what is assessed must be aligned for student achievement to increase.

In conversations with teachers about student evaluations, administrators should include suggestions for combining a variety of formal and informal assessments. Administrators also should emphasize the importance of high-level teaching and not just skill and drill (see *Evidence-Based Reading Instruction: Putting the National Reading Panel Report Into Practice* [IRA, 2002a] for examples of high-level teaching strategies). In his book *The Case Against Standardized Testing: Raising the Scores, Ruining the Schools* (2000), Kohn argues that students have been drilled relentlessly to raise test scores, leading to dull classrooms and an overall impoverished education. Instructional leaders should have high expectations for each student's success and provide support and encouragement that will assist teachers in achieving those expectations.

Supporting and Encouraging Teachers

Administrators ultimately might be responsible for school improvement, but teachers are the ones who will make that improvement happen. Therefore, effective administrators understand the importance of catching teachers doing good things and recognizing their efforts. When visiting classrooms, administrators should have paper or sticky notes readily available so they can provide immediate feedback upon observing teachers implementing best literacy practices. This technique also can be employed as a way to provide ideas and suggestions regarding additional resources to strengthen and support an observed lesson. Support and encouragement also can be demonstrated through weekly memos to the staff celebrating the successes of individual teachers by sharing specific literacy practices that teachers have effectively implemented. Exemplary literacy teachers also can be invited by administrators to serve as mentors to new and less experienced teachers. Above all, to support their teachers, administrators must be visible, positive, and knowledgeable. When teachers feel supported and encouraged, they are more motivated and enthusiastic about implementing new strategies and techniques.

Developing Teacher Leaders

A strong literacy program requires leadership in instruction. According to Lezotte (2004), instructional leadership is one of the correlates of effective schools. Lezotte asserts that first-generation correlates of instructional leadership focus on the principal and administrative staff and second-generation correlates are broadened to include teachers. Thus, the role of administrators changes from being leaders of followers to leaders of leaders. Lezotte states that "a principal cannot be the only leader in a complex organization like a school" (p. 76). Broadening the leadership base to include teachers does not remove the administrator from being the instructional leader; it accentuates the need to model what a good administrator should be.

Teachers identified to be teacher leaders should be excellent teachers with in-depth knowledge of reading instruction and assessment as well as exemplary teaching skills. Administrators at all levels are responsible for assisting teachers in becoming leaders. Ongoing opportunities for professional development and support are essential for teacher leaders to be successful. Conversations with identified teachers will help determine what professional development teachers may need to improve their overall skills and knowledge. Recognizing teachers as leaders can be a catalyst for moving hesitant teachers forward as they serve as role models and facilitate in-service sessions for their peers. McAndrew (2005) offers practical advice for literacy professionals interested in improving their leadership skills, including information on the barriers to and successes of teacher leadership as well as creating new leaders.

Understanding all aspects of the instructional program can be a daunting undertaking for any administrator; therefore, teacher leaders can be an invaluable resource. As Fullan (2001) states, "Ultimately, your leadership in a culture of change will be judged as effective or ineffective not by who you are as a leader but by what leadership you produce in others" (p. 137).

Serving as an Instructional Resource for Staff

Effective instructional leaders in literacy should be exemplary teachers of literacy. In *The Literacy Principal* (2002), Booth and Rowsell support educator Shelley Harwayne's belief that principals are teachers and that literacy is a significant part of the principal's role. Administrators must not only be knowledgeable of effective reading methods but also skilled in implementing those practices. This level of understanding enables them to be able to provide feedback and suggestions to teachers as they implement new policies, programs, and strategies.

Administrators who are instructional leaders in literacy should have bookshelves in their offices filled with all types of literature, including books they can share with parents, students, and teachers. To promote literacy and learning among staff members, administrators can choose to organize a book club for teachers and administrators. Selected books should include children's books (fiction and nonfiction), adult books, and professional resource books. In addition, research suggests that when administrators are involved in the practice of teaching and serve as models in the classroom, staff members perceive them as an example of strong instructional leadership (Allington & Cunningham, 2002; Blasé & Blasé, 2000; McEwan, 2002). Whether reading stories, demonstrating teaching strategies, or observing teachers, administrators' visibility sends the message that they are an instructional resource and they support high-quality instruction.

Schools and districts with successful literacy programs have instructional leaders that value reading, promote best literacy practices, and find time to conduct conversations with teachers about best literacy practices. To be a strong instructional leader who can talk to teachers about issues of instruction and professional development, administrators must possess a basic understanding of reading instruction.

What Administrators Need to Know About Reading Instruction

Improving student performance involves a number of factors. According to the National Reading Panel Report of 2000 (NRP; National Institute of Child Health and Human Development [NICHD]), it is not specific programs that are most effective in improving student achievement; rather, it is the use of effective practices. The NRP summarized several decades of research on reading instruction that helped identify the five essential components of effective reading instruction as incorporated into NCLB and Reading First initiatives: (1) phonemic awareness, (2) phonics, (3) vocabulary development, (4) fluency, and (5) comprehension. Administrators need to be knowledgeable in these areas and understand the importance of attending to other key elements that make a sound literacy program, such as oral language development, writing, motivation, assistance to struggling readers, and literacy coaches. Administrators not only need to be aware of these components but also need to understand the related research and instructional strategies for successful implementation.

According to the IRA position statement *What is Evidenced-Based Reading Instruction?* (2002b), the following criteria should be considered when reviewing research on reading programs and practices: The research should be based on more than one study; include a convergence of evidence from a variety of study designs, including observational studies; and reflect no evidence of conflict of interest. Making decisions about which research-based reading programs and practices to implement can be overwhelming. Therefore, administrators should involve a large number of stakeholders when reviewing the research and making decisions. Mazzoni and Gambrell (2003) also provide insight into items that administrators should consider when reviewing reading programs and practices. They argue that all methods should

- teach reading through authentic, meaning-making literacy experiences for pleasure, to be informed, and to perform a task;
- use high-quality literature;
- integrate a comprehensive word study/phonics program into reading/writing instruction;
- use multiple texts that link and expand concepts;
- balance teacher- and student-led discussions;
- build a whole-class community that emphasizes important concepts and builds background knowledge;

- work with students in small groups while other students read and write about what they have read;
- give students plenty of time to read in class;
- give students explicit instruction in decoding and comprehension strategies that promote independent reading;
- balance direct instruction, guided instruction, and independent learning; and
- use a variety of assessment techniques to inform instruction. (p. 14)

Effective instructional leaders have a strong knowledge base of current research-based literacy strategies and can effectively communicate and work with teachers to select and implement these practices. In addition to being knowledgeable about sound literacy practices, a good administrator also recognizes other school characteristics that can impact student achievement.

Characteristics of Schools That Have an Effect on Achievement

There are numerous characteristics of achieving schools, including leadership; however, leadership is not only essential for schools' achievement but also for improved reading achievement. Booth and Rowsell (2002) report that schools with successful literacy programs show evidence of strong administrative leadership as well as some additional characteristics. The more information administrators have about characteristics that improve schools and reading achievement, the greater the chance of meeting the goals of NCLB and Reading First.

In *Portraits of Six Benchmark Schools: Developing Approaches to Improving School Achievement*, Cawelti (1999) identifies the following common characteristics of achieving schools:

- focus on clear standards and on improving results,
- teamwork to ensure accountability,
- principal as a strong educational leader,
- teachers deeply committed to helping all students achieve, and
- openness to changes needed to improve instruction. (p. 3)

It is interesting to note that most of the items are reflected in the research on schools with effective literacy programs as cited by Pikulski

(2003) in his keynote address at the 48th IRA Annual Convention. Pikulski discussed the following school characteristics as making a difference in reading achievement:

- teacher capability,
- instructional leadership,
- sound early literacy programs, and
- appropriate reading interventions.

These two sources use different terminology in reference to the role of the administrator; however, whether the word *educational* or *instructional* is used, the concept is basically the same—providing leadership that will improve classroom instruction. Administrators who are knowledgeable about reading instruction and who have a positive literacy agenda are major contributors to successful students and higher achieving schools.

Conclusion

Students deserve access to the best possible instruction, provided by the most qualified teachers. Evidence strongly supports the role of administrators as instructional leaders. According to Fullan and Hargreaves (1996), when a school has one or two bad teachers, it is usually a problem with the individual teachers. When a school has many bad teachers, it is a problem of leadership. The primary work of the school administrator must be to improve classroom instruction (Allington, 2001).

Administrators who are effective instructional leaders, whether at the school or district level, can make a difference. However, making this difference requires commitment, time, and energy. Administrators must have a clear understanding of what definitive research is, know what the components of a comprehensive literacy program are, and be familiar with the factors that contribute to being a strong and effective instructional leader in literacy. This knowledge and understanding will help them provide the leadership necessary for school achievement to improve.

Allington and Cunningham (2002) suggest that "administrators need to ask not, 'Are we doing something?' but, 'Are we doing the right things?'" (p. 87). Administrators who possess knowledge of instructional content and appropriate strategies for teaching that content are better able to work with teachers to do the right things to ensure that all students experience reading success.

REFERENCES

Allington, R.L. (2001). *What really matters for struggling readers: Designing research-based programs*. New York: Longman.

Allington, R.L., & Cunningham, P.M. (2002). *Schools that work: Where all children read and write* (2nd ed.). Boston: Allyn & Bacon.

Blasé, J., & Blasé, J. (2000). Effective instructional leadership: Teachers' perspectives on how principals promote teaching and learning in schools. *Journal of Educational Administration, 38*(2), 130–141.

Booth, D., & Rowsell, J. (2002). *The literacy principal: Leading, assessing, and supporting reading and writing initiatives*. Markham, ON: Pembroke.

Cawelti, G. (1999). *Portraits of six benchmark schools: Developing approaches to improving school achievement*. Arlington, VA: Educational Research Service.

Deal, T.E., & Peterson, K.D. (1994). *The leadership paradox: Balancing logic and artistry in schools*. San Francisco: Jossey-Bass.

Fullan, M. (2001). *Leading in a culture of change*. San Francisco: Jossey-Bass.

Fullan, M., & Hargreaves, A. (1996). *What's worth fighting for in your school*. New York: Teachers College Press.

International Reading Association (IRA). (2000). *Making a difference means making it different: Honoring children's rights to excellent reading instruction* (Position statement). Newark, DE: Author.

International Reading Association (IRA). (2002a). *Evidence-based reading instruction: Putting the National Reading Panel report into practice*. Newark, DE: Author.

International Reading Association (IRA). (2002b). *What is evidence-based reading instruction?* (Position statement). Newark, DE: Author.

Kohn, A. (2000). *The case against standardized testing: Raising the scores, ruining the schools*. Portsmouth, NH: Heinemann.

Lezotte, L.W. (2004). *Learning for all* (Rev. ed.). Okemos, MI: Effective Schools Products, Ltd.

Mazzoni, S.A., & Gambrell, S. (2003). Principles of best practices: Finding the common ground. In L.M. Morrow, L.B. Gambrell, A.B. Neuman, & M. Pressley (Eds.), *Best practices in literacy instruction* (2nd ed., pp. 9–21). New York: Guilford.

McAndrew, D.A. (2005). *Literacy leadership: Six strategies for peoplework*. Newark, DE: International Reading Association.

McEwan, E.K. (2002). *7 steps to effective instructional leadership*. Thousand Oaks, CA: Sage.

National Institute of Child Health and Human Development. (2000). *Report of the National Reading Panel. Teaching children to read: An evidence-based assessment of the scientific research literature on reading and its implications for reading instruction* (NIH Publication No. 00-4769). Washington, DC: U.S. Government Printing Office.

No Child Left Behind Act of 2001, Pub. L. No. 107-110, 115 Stat. 1425 (2002). Retrieved October 1, 2005, from http://edworkforce.house.gov/issues/107th/education/nclb/nclb.htm

Pikulski, J.J. (2003, May). *What really makes a difference in reading*. Keynote address presented at the International Reading Association 48th Annual Convention, Orlando, FL.

CHAPTER 2

Phonemic Awareness: Activities That Make Sounds Come Alive

Billie J. Enz

RIDING IN THE CAR, 4-year-old Jeremy belts out, "Spiderman, Spiderman, if he can't save us, no one can." The impromptu song is triggered as Jeremy and his mom pass by a giant Spiderman poster gracing the front of a shopping mall. Pleased with his song, Jeremy begins to play with the words, "Spidey, bitey, mighty, tighty, nighty." Laughing, Jeremy sings out another slightly altered chorus, "Tightyman, Tightyman, if he can't save us, no one can." .

A t age 4, Jeremy is well on the way to becoming a reader. His growing skills at recognizing logographic print (i.e., the Spiderman poster), substituting initial sounds, and hearing rhyming words indicate that he is developing the early building blocks of literacy. Jeremy's ability to hear these sounds is the beginning of phonological awareness, or the capacity to deal explicitly and segmentally with sound units smaller than a syllable. Awareness at the level of the phoneme has particular significance for the acquisition of reading literacy because of its role in the development of the alphabetic principle (Stanovich, 1993–1994). Although Jeremy has an implicit knowledge of the sounds

Understanding and Implementing Reading First Initiatives: The Changing Role of Administrators by Carrice Cummins, Editor. Copyright © 2006 by the International Reading Association.

of his language, to become a fluent reader and writer, Jeremy (and every child) needs to develop an explicit understanding of the alphabetic principle; that is, they need to know the following:

- Sentences are composed of individual words.
- Words are composed of combinations of individual letters.
- Letters have a relation with phonemes (smallest sounds of speech).

The National Reading Panel Report of 2000 (NRP; National Institute of Child Health and Human Development [NICHD]) provides insight into the skills considered to be most directly linked to early success in reading, which includes phonemic awareness. Administrators engaged in implementing Reading First—a part of the No Child Left Behind Act of 2001 (2002)—programs and strategies are often called on to offer guidance and advice to teachers who are continually developing their practices in these areas. Therefore, administrators must be familiar with phonemic awareness and be able to offer examples of ways teachers can most effectively and appropriately provide students opportunities to learn and hone this skill.

Defining Phonemic Awareness

Phonemes are the smallest sounds in spoken words, and they affect a word's meaning. For example, changing the first phoneme in the word *cat* from /c/ to /h/ changes the word from *cat* to *hat* which, of course, changes the word's meaning. Phonemic awareness is the ability to notice, think about, and work with the individual sounds in spoken words. Before most children learn to read print, they need to become aware of how the sounds in words work. They must understand that words are made up of speech sounds, or phonemes.

Like Jeremy, most children usually demonstrate their understanding of phonemic awareness informally and in playful situations. They play with the sounds of their language by using alliteration, experimenting with rhyming words, and hyper-articulating words. However, this informal knowledge is often insufficient to help them in the formal reading process. The purpose of phonemic awareness instruction is to help children learn to hear and manipulate these sounds consistently and effortlessly.

Administrators should be aware that although phonemic awareness is a widely used term in reading, it is often misunderstood. Phonemic awareness is *not* phonics. Phonemic awareness is the understanding that the sounds of *spoken* language work together to make words. Phonics, on the other hand, refers to the predictable relation between phonemes and graphemes, the letters that represent those sounds in *written* language. If children are to benefit from phonics instruction, they need phonemic awareness (Armbruster, Lehr, & Osborn, 2001).

Phonemic Awareness and Reading Development: Predictive Factor, Consequence, or Reciprocal Relation?

As with most issues dealing with reading instruction, educators have divergent views of the role phonemic awareness plays in helping children learn to read. One view is that children's level of phonemic awareness is one of the strongest predictors of success in learning to read. In fact, some research suggests phonemic awareness accounts for 50% of the variance in children's reading proficiency at the end of first grade (Adams, Beeler, Foorman, & Lundberg, 1998). Conversely, other researchers have argued that phonemic awareness may be a consequence or an artifact of learning to read, rather than a causal factor in its development (Cunningham, 1990; Krashen, 2001a, 2001b). However, there is an increasing consensus that the data are best explained by considering the relation between phonemic awareness and reading development as a reciprocal one (Stanovich, 1993–1994). A threshold phonemic awareness level may be necessary (although not sufficient) for beginning reading development, but as reading ability develops children increasingly become more sensitive to phonemes and thus better able to manipulate sounds. Hence, some researchers say that phonemic awareness is both a prerequisite for and a consequence of learning to read (Yopp, 1992). Therefore, administrators need to help primary-grade teachers see phonemic awareness instruction as necessary for children's growing literacy skills.

Teaching Phonemic Awareness

Clearly, phonemic awareness plays an important role in helping children become fluent readers; however, acquisition of phonemic awareness is not guaranteed simply through maturation. In fact, about one third of students require varying degrees of assistance to promote its development (Adams, 1990). Hence, it is important to consider the best way to introduce and reinforce phonemic awareness. Yopp (1992) offers the following recommendations for teaching phonemic awareness activities:

- Keep a sense of playfulness and fun; avoid drill and rote memorization.

- Use group settings that encourage interaction among children.

- Encourage children's curiosity about language and their experimentation with it.

As administrators work with primary-grade teachers, it is important to consider the length of young children's attention spans; therefore, it is better to only spend a few minutes each day engaging preschool, kindergarten, and first-grade children in activities that emphasize the sounds of language. A few minutes several times a day helps maintain students' interests and enthusiasm and provides the necessary repetition without the feeling of being drilled (Vukelich, Christie, & Enz, 2002). The following phonemic awareness strategies—sound isolation, rhyme, onsets and rimes—can be presented using environmental print, songs, poems, and children's literature as the meaningful contexts. The actual activities should employ developmentally appropriate, explicit instruction and guidelines suggested by Yopp (1992) and the NRP report (NICHD, 2000).

Sound Isolation

Although there are 26 letters in the English language, there are approximately 40 phonemes, or sound units. The sounds of the English language are represented in 250 different spellings (e.g., /f/ as in *ph—phone, f—fall, gh—enough,* and *ff—baffle*). Likewise, the sounds that make up words are coarticulated; that is, the sounds are usually blended together and are not distinctly separate from each other. Hence, one of the first goals of phonemic awareness is to help children hear the distinct sounds of the letters. The following vignette demonstrates how Mrs. Martinez, a preschool teacher, uses the children's current interests and prior knowledge to begin a sound isolation activity.

"I can read this," says nearly 4-year-old Eufemia as she holds up a colorful paper plate. "It says 'Pokémon.' I got it at a birthday party for my cousin yesterday." Ms. Martinez responds, "Yes, Eufemia. It says 'Pokémon.'"

Ms. Martinez is always amazed at her preschoolers' abilities to recognize the print in their environment. To capitalize on their prior knowledge and help them learn to hear initial sounds, Ms. Martinez has created an Environmental Print "I Can Read" Chart (see Figure 2.1). There already are about 30 logos on the

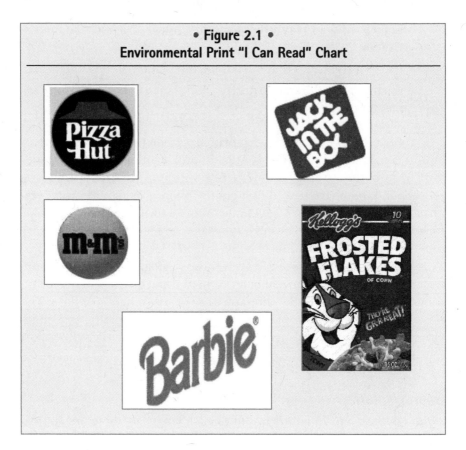

• Figure 2.1 •
Environmental Print "I Can Read" Chart

chart, and the children bring in new objects or wrappers daily. Ms. Martinez says the word, "Pppppokémon," and as she pronounces the word, she hyper-articulates the initial sound. She asks the children to say it with her.

The following day, in the few minutes before the children leave for home, Ms. Martinez plays a phonemic awareness reinforcement game similar to Hot or Cold, a game in which students use the volume of their voices to indicate that the student is close to or far from the object. She takes the Pokémon plate off the chart and sends Martin outside. When Martin is outside, she hides the plate behind the large wooden clock in the front of the room. As she brings Martin inside, his classmates begin to quietly chant /ppp/. As Martin moves toward the front of the room, the other preschoolers begin to increase the volume at which they say /ppp/. Taking his cues from the volume of the chants, Martin turns left. Suddenly, the volume drops to a whisper, so he knows he has gone astray. Turning around, he spots the target. As he quickly moves to pick up the Pokémon plate, the children yell /PPP/.

Ms. Martinez's intentional use of the Environmental Print "I Can Read" Chart helps teach and reinforce the children's knowledge of print and the initial sounds the words make. This activity also draws on the students' current interests in and prior knowledge of the print in their homes and neighborhoods (Enz et al., 2003). Similar to the chart, in just a few minutes a day, the Hot or Cold game provides the needed repetition to learn a new skill—phonemic awareness—but without a boring or stressful drill.

In the preschool classroom next door to Ms. Martinez, Ms. Sullivan uses songs to help children isolate initial sounds. For instance, to teach them the sound /f/, she introduces them to the song "Shoo, Fly, Don't Bother Me." After the children have learned the song, Ms. Sullivan asks them to focus on the first sound of the word *fly*. The teacher and children make the sound /f/ and stretch the sound. Then, they sing the song as follows:

Shoo, Fly, Don't Bother Me
Shoo, ffffly, don't bother me
Shoo, ffffly, don't bother me
Shoo, ffffly, don't bother me
Ffffor I belong to somebody
I ffffeel, I ffffeel,
I ffffeel like a morning star,
I ffffeel, I ffffeel,
I fffffeel like a morning star.

The next day, Mrs. Sullivan and the children sing the song again, but this time she asks the children to clap their hands when they hear /f/. Initially, this activity is difficult for some students, but after a few tries, the class has mastered the skill.

The following day, Mrs. Sullivan and the students sing the song again, but this time Mrs. Sullivan focuses on the /b/ sound. As the students sing the song, Ms. Sullivan hyperarticulates the /b/ in *bother*. Next, she asks the students to stamp their feet when they hear the /b/ sound.

The next week, Mrs. Sullivan varies this activity by dividing the class in half. One half of the class claps when they hear the /f/ sound, and the other half stomps their feet when they hear the /b/ sound. The students enjoy this activity and ask to do it frequently.

Mrs. Sullivan and her class continue to learn and play with this song and many other songs for several weeks, spending a few minutes focusing on different initial sounds each time. By winter break, most of

Mrs. Sullivan's 18 four-year-old students have learned to hear the initial sounds of words. She also has noticed that they are playing with different letter sounds on their own when they sing songs at free play in the music center.

Mrs. Sullivan's sound isolation activities engaged all the children and helped them learn to hear the initial sounds of words in a developmentally appropriate manner. In addition, the children were able to isolate sounds on their own in the music center, which demonstrates how the ability to isolate sounds is transferable to other situations. There are many other effective activities teachers can use to help children develop phonemic awareness skills, such as in the following example.

> To help his kindergarten students isolate and discriminate initial letter sounds, Mr. Riggs plays a sound sort game. He uses 4-by-5-inch drawings or pictures of common objects. Today, he is focusing on the letter sound /b/. He shows the students four pictures (see Figure 2.2) and asks them to tell him what each

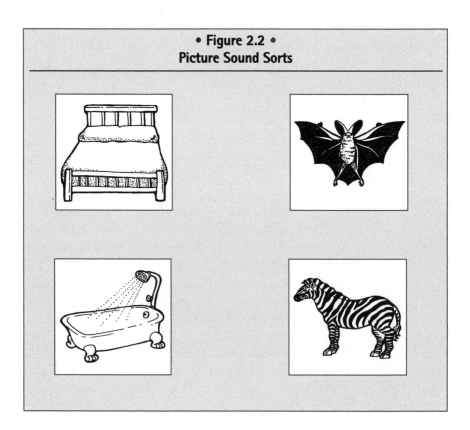

• Figure 2.2 •
Picture Sound Sorts

picture is. As the students respond, Mr. Riggs repeats what they say, but he elaborates and sustains the initial sound—for example, b-b-b-bed. He tells the students that he needs them to be sound detectives. They need to find the picture that does not start with the /b/ sound. After the students correctly identify the zebra, he adds new pictures—some that start with /b/ and some that have different initial sounds. The students play the sound sort game for several minutes each day.

Mr. Riggs's playful approach to hearing and discriminating sounds allows his students to develop this critical skill with little risk of failure. Further, because the students actually demonstrate their ability to hear and discriminate sounds through their sorting of the cards, Mr. Riggs can assess their growing skills and abilities while they play the game, thus eliminating the need to conduct more formal tests.

Rhyme

The ability to recognize rhyme may be the entry point to phonemic awareness development for many children (Hatcher, Hulme, & Ellis, 1994). To be aware that words can have a similar end-sound is a critical step in phonemic development. There is considerable evidence indicating that sensitivity to rhyme makes both a direct and indirect contribution to reading (Mann, 1993; Yopp, 1992). Directly, it helps students appreciate that words that share common sounds usually share common letter sequences. Indirectly, the child's subsequent sensitivity to common letter sequences then makes a significant contribution to reading strategy development.

To help his students hear and see rhymes, Mr. Riggs uses familiar children's poems and jump-rope chants.

Today, Mr. Riggs is teaching his student the poem "Teddy Bear, Teddy Bear." After they learn the poem and the accompanying motions for it, Mr. Riggs presents the poem to the children on an enlarged laminated chart.

Teddy Bear, Teddy Bear
Teddy bear, Teddy bear, touch the ground.
Teddy bear, Teddy bear, turn around.
Teddy bear, Teddy bear, blow out the light.
Teddy bear, Teddy bear, say good night.

After they read the poem together, Mr. Riggs asks the children to reread the poem in pairs and see if they hear any words that sound alike. One pair thinks *ground* and *around* sound alike. The rest of the class agrees. Another pair thinks that *night* and *light* sound alike. Again, the rest of the class nods in agreement. Mr. Riggs tells them that words that sound alike at the end are called rhyming words.

The following day, Mr. Riggs has the class do a choral rereading of "Teddy Bear, Teddy Bear." He asks the class, "Do you remember what we call words that sound alike?" The children respond, "Rhyme." He tells them that the book he is going to read them is filled with rhymes, and he asks them to listen carefully. Then, he reads the first page of Dr. Seuss's book *There's a Wocket in My Pocket* (1974): "Did you ever have the feeling there's a ZAMP in the LAMP?"

As he reads the page, his kindergartners laugh at the silly nonsense word rhyme. After Mr. Riggs reads the book, he goes back through it, and as the children begin to identify the rhymes, he writes them down.

nink—sink
woset—closet
certain—jertain—curtain
tock—zlock—clock
zelf—shelf—myself

As Mr. Riggs writes, the children make the discovery that the rhyming words have the same letters at the end—that they are spelled alike. For the next several days, Mr. Riggs reads books that feature rhymes. In addition to reading the stories, the class also helps Mr. Riggs identify the rhyming words. After a few days, the class becomes adept at hearing rhyming words.

Again, the activity Mr. Riggs uses is playful in nature. It allows the students to learn to hear and see rhymes with immediate verbal and visual reinforcement. Because Mr. Riggs has focus lessons on rhyming words over several reading lessons, he offers students many opportunities to practice hearing rhymes and also gives them a chance to see the letter and word families that make the rhymes. This, in turn, helps prepare students to move toward the next step of learning to read—the alphabetic principle.

Onsets and Rimes

Onsets and rimes, sometimes referred to as word families or word patterns, are perhaps the easiest way to help children begin the decoding process. An onset is the initial consonant sound(s) of a syllable (e.g., the onset of *cat* is /c/; *stop*, /st/), and the part of the syllable that contains the vowel and all that follows is called the rime (e.g., the letters *at* in *cat*, *hat*, and *sat*; *op* in *stop*). As children are able to isolate sounds and hear rhymes, they can often begin to manipulate letter sounds to make words. This process of putting together letters and articulating their sounds is called blending. Once children start to become familiar with the concept, teachers can introduce letter tiles, squares, or magnetic letters and let children use these manipulatives to blend sounds into words (NICHD, 2000; Vukelich et al., 2002). Although phonemic awareness is an auditory skill, teachers can increase children's understanding of the alphabetic principle when the manipulation of letter symbols is added to phonemic awareness tasks (NICHD, 2000). The following example from Ms. Tolan's kindergarten class illustrates this process.

By October, Ms. Tolan's kindergartners are quickly becoming familiar with letter sounds and symbols. She has been reading dozens of books that feature rhymes. Today, she is introducing her students to word families (rimes and onsets). She begins by reading one of her students' favorite books, *Jake Baked the Cake* (Hennesy & Morgan-Vanroyen, 1990). She asks the students to identify some of the rhyming words they hear. Of course, the first words the children list are *Jake*, *bake*, and *cake*.

Ms. Tolan isolates the *ake* rime. She asks the children to say the word family *ake* with her. She asks the children what would happen if she added the sound /m/ to the word family. The children and Ms. Tolan blend the sounds /m/ and *ake*. She writes the new word *make* on the board. Next, she asks the children to consider what would happen if they added the sound /t/ to the rime. This time, they blend the sounds /t/ and *ake*. Then, Ms. Tolan adds the word *take* to the list and congratulates the children on their efforts.

The following day, Ms. Tolan asks the children to work in pairs, and she gives each pair a set of magnetic letters and a magnetic board (actually a small, inexpensive cookie pan). She asks the children to look at the list of words they read yesterday. The children quickly read the words that Ms. Tolan has placed on the *ake* family word wall, an interactive bulletin board that displays words the children are learning to recognize.

Jake
baked
cake
make
take

Ms. Tolan asks the children to work together to make one of the *ake* family words using the magnetic letters. She circulates among the children to see if they are able to make the words. After the children make their *ake* words, she asks them to share with the group what word they have made. Next, Ms. Tolan asks the children to think of what letters would make up the word *rake*. The children quickly start to make the /r/ sound, and they begin to hunt for the magnetic letter *r*. Ms. Tolan asks the children to check one another's work as she writes the word *rake* on the *ake* family word wall. Finally, she asks the children to listen carefully and find the letters that make *fake*.

Over the next few weeks, Ms. Tolan uses similar procedures to begin to introduce the 37 most common phonograms and some of the 500 words they make up. She only uses this exercise, which the children call the Make a Word Game, for about 10 minutes each day. The feeling of fun this game engenders is critical to the children's sense of excitement when this phonemic awareness and early phonics activity is used in Ms. Tolan's class.

The ability to recognize onsets and rimes is an important step forward for children, and it connects phonemic awareness to phonic instruction. After children have had plenty of opportunities to sound out letters in words, they come to recognize rimes as familiar spelling patterns. Then, children are able to recognize patterns without sounding them out. Therefore, this quick recognition of rimes is a natural consequence of sounding out letters in words. Ultimately, children's ability to identify rimes helps them read more rapidly.

Conclusion

Over the past decade there has been increasing consensus about what factors contribute to reading success and failure. Reviews by Hurford et al. (1993), Mann (1993), and the NRP (NICHD, 2000) have noted that the presence or absence of phonemic awareness instruction appears to be a factor that discriminates good readers from poor readers.

The NRP's report (NICHD, 2000) strongly recommends that, whenever possible, phonemic awareness instruction also be connected to alphabet recognition because this combination appears to further enhance alphabetic understanding. A child's ability to easily recognize the smallest units of speech and quickly and consistently connect them with their symbolic representations (i.e., letters) allows that child to develop reading fluency (Stanovich, 1986). In addition, there have been a number of longitudinal studies that demonstrate that the relation between phonemic awareness and reading progress is causal (Ehri, 1998; Stanovich, 1986). In a number of these studies, the teaching of phonemic awareness has occurred in conjunction with letter–sound instruction (Hatcher et al., 1994). Children in programs that use both sound and symbol instruction demonstrate greater improvement in reading than those exposed to a solely oral phonemic awareness program. Researchers Liberman, Shankweiler, and Liberman (1989) suggest that the reason for this advantage lies with the manner in which phonemic awareness provides a marker to beginning readers that there is a logic to the reading process. Again, reinforcing the reciprocal view of phonemic awareness, Ehri (1998) suggests that it is not until students appreciate how our alphabet is designed to represent speech that most phonemic awareness development occurs.

Research indicates that phonological awareness can be taught and that students who increased their awareness of phonemes facilitated their subsequent reading acquisition (Spector, 1995). Using developmentally appropriate, explicit instructional activities is a highly effective means for teaching children to hear discrete phonemes. This instructional approach ultimately helps children connect letters to sounds, and the decoding process becomes easier.

REFERENCES

Adams, M.J. (1990). *Beginning to read: Thinking and learning about print.* Cambridge, MA: MIT Press.

Adams, M.J., Beeler, T., Foorman, B.R., & Lundberg, I. (1998). *Phonemic awareness in young children: A classroom curriculum.* Baltimore: Paul H. Brookes.

Armbruster, B.B., Lehr, F., & Osborn, J. (2001). *Put reading first: The research building blocks for teaching children to read.* Washington, DC: Partnership for Reading.

Cunningham, A.E. (1990). Explicit versus implicit instruction in phonemic awareness. *Journal of Experimental Child Psychology, 50*(3), 429–444.

Ehri, L. (1998). Presidential address. In J.P. Williams (Ed.), *Scientific studies of reading Vol. 2 #2* (pp. 97–114). Mahwah, NJ: Erlbaum.

Enz, B.J., Christie, J., Han, M., Gerard, M., Prior, J., & Xu, S. (2003). *Examining environmental print as a learning tool in diverse primary classrooms.* Paper presented at the National Reading Conference, Phoenix, AZ.

Hatcher, P., Hulme, C., & Ellis, A. (1994). Ameliorating reading failure by integrating the teaching of reading and phonological skills: The phonological linkage hypothesis. *Child Development, 65*(1), 41–57.

Hurford, D.P., Darrow, L., Edwards, T., Howerton, C., Mote, C., Schauf, J., et al. (1993). An examination of phonemic processing abilities in children during their first-grade year. *Journal of Learning Disabilities, 26*(3), 167–177.

Krashen, S. (2001a). Low PA can read OK. *Practically Primary, 6*(3), 17–20.

Krashen, S. (2001b). More smoke and mirrors: A critique of the National Reading Panel report on fluency. *Phi Delta Kappan, 83*(2), 119–123.

Liberman, I.Y., Shankweiler, D., & Liberman, A.M. (1989). The alphabetic principle and learning to read. In D. Shankweiler & I.Y. Liberman (Eds.), *Phonology and reading disability: Solving the reading puzzle* (pp. 1–33). Ann Arbor: University of Michigan Press.

Mann, V.A. (1993). Phoneme awareness and future reading ability. *Journal of Learning Disabilities, 26*(4), 259–269.

National Institute of Child Health and Human Development (NICHD). (2000). *Report of the National Reading Panel. Teaching children to read: An evidence-based assessment of the scientific research literature on reading and its implications for reading instruction* (NIH Publication No. 00-4769). Washington, DC: U.S. Government Printing Office.

No Child Left Behind Act of 2001, Pub. L. No. 107-110, 115 Stat. 1425 (2002). Retrieved October 1, 2005, from http://edworkforce.house.gov/issues/107th/education/nclb/nclb.htm

Spector, J.E. (1995). Phonemic awareness training: Application of principles of direct instruction. *Reading and Writing Quarterly: Overcoming Learning Difficulties, 11*(1), 37–52.

Stanovich, K.E. (1986). Matthew effects in reading: Some consequences of individual differences in the acquisition of literacy. *Reading Research Quarterly, 21,* 360–407.

Stanovich, K.E. (1993–1994). Romance and reality (Distinguished Educator Series). *The Reading Teacher, 47*(4), 280–291.

Vukelich, C., Christie, J., & Enz, B.J. (2002). *Helping young children learn language and literacy.* Boston: Allyn & Bacon.

Yopp, H.K. (1992). Developing phonemic awareness in young children. *The Reading Teacher, 45*(9), 696–703.

LITERATURE CITED

Dr. Seuss. (1974). *There's a wocket in my pocket.* New York: Random House.

Hennesy, B.G., & Morgan-Vanroyen, M. (1990). *Jake baked the cake.* New York: Viking Penguin.

CHAPTER 3

Phonics: Explicit and Meaningful Instruction

Lesley Mandel Morrow and Heather Morgan

MRS. MORGAN'S first-grade class is studying initial consonant sounds and connecting them to their letter symbols. Mrs. Morgan has done explicit lessons for many letters and is now focusing on *m*, *t*, and *s*. The children identify the letters and sounds and look for them in their names, in print around the classroom, and at home.

To connect this more explicit instruction to a meaningful context, they talk about the letters and sounds as they relate to their unit on the community. Mrs. Morgan places a large map of the town in which they live on an easel. She connects the theme and the letters by using keywords in the unit: *m* for map, *t* for town, and *s* for school. She uses books such as *Town Mouse and Country Mouse* (Brett, 1994) to introduce the letters and connect them with the theme. Mrs. Morgan encourages the students to create their own stories about the town using the featured letters—for example, Molly and Mike Moved and Six Silly Snakes Slithered to School—and to locate objects in the room that begin with the featured letters.

As Ryan and Adasha are staring at the map, Ryan says, "I see the Target store. Let's look for other places on the map that begin with the letter *t*." They find Town Hall, Taft Street, Tommy's Restaurant, and Toys "R" Us. They are excited about their discovery and pronounce each word with a strong emphasis on the

Understanding and Implementing Reading First Initiatives: The Changing Role of Administrators by Carrice Cummins, Editor. Copyright © 2006 by the International Reading Association.

beginning /t/, as Mrs. Morgan had demonstrated many times. In an activity for the whole class, Mrs. Morgan has the students write the street names that begin with the targeted letters, and she focuses on a different letter each day.

Teaching phonics involves children learning letter sounds and their related symbols. Attention to phonics instruction has fluctuated over the years, with renewed attention being at an all-time high due to the No Child Left Behind Act of 2001 (2002) and the National Reading Panel Report of 2000 (National Institute of Child Health and Human Development). According to the report, which studied completed scientific research on reading instruction, learning phonics is a strong predictor of reading success. For this reason, phonics is identified as one of five essential components of effective reading instruction. Consequently, administrators need to understand not only how phonics instruction should be taught but also how it fits within other reading instructional elements, for example, as in the themed unit on community described in the vignette at the beginning of the chapter.

Phonics is just one part of teaching reading; it is often given more emphasis than is necessary at the expense of other reading skills. A basic understanding of phonics instruction can help assist administrators in working with teachers in designing phonics instruction that accommodates students' individual needs.

Defining Phonics Instruction

Phonics instruction teaches children that letter sounds and combinations of letter sounds (phonemes) are associated with corresponding letter symbols (graphemes). Phonics instruction shows children the relations between the phonemes and graphemes and how to use these relations to read and write words. In phonics instruction, children learn the sound–symbol relations of consonants, long and short vowels, digraphs (such as *ch*, *sh*, and *th*), blends (such as *cl*, *tr*, or *str*), irregular patterns, and so forth (Armbruster, Lehr, & Osborn, 2001). According to Stahl (1992), good phonics instruction should help make sense of the patterns within words.

To be able to identify sound–symbol relations, students must develop phonological awareness (see chapter 2), which is the ability to recognize that words are made up of individual sounds. Children learn to hear sounds, identify their associated letters, and match and create patterns, such as rhymes, in words. To make sound–symbol relations, children also must be able to segment and blend words. They must be able to segment the onset, or beginning sound of a word, and then blend it to the ending group of letters, called a rime, phonogram, or word family. If this is done with the word *hat*, for example, the child should be able to say /h/ for the onset *h* and then /at/ for the rime *at*. After segmenting the word, the child should be able to blend it together again to say the entire word *hat*.

The goal of phonics instruction is for children to become independent readers when they come across unknown words. To decode such words, they need to be able to (a) identify individual sounds and patterns of sounds in a word, (b) identify symbols associated with the sounds in a word, (c) know the number of sounds heard, and (d) blend the word together.

A major concern about phonics is that English spellings are quite irregular, which may make it difficult for phonics instruction to help children to read independently (Armbruster et al., 2001). However, studies have shown that explicit and systematic teaching of phonics is more effective in children's growth than nonsystematic or no phonics instruction (Armbruster et al., 2001). Given that research has found the importance of phonics knowledge as a strong predictor of successful early reading, we can no longer debate whether or not phonics instruction is important; rather, we need to discuss which approaches to teaching phonics are most effective and how much time to spend teaching phonics (Morrow & Tracey, 1997). What does this mean for teaching phonics?

Teaching Phonics

As previously mentioned, phonics instruction is one component of the reading process, and it can be taught in explicit ways and within meaningful contexts. Research has found the importance of meaningful contexts in early literacy instruction (Morrow, 2005; Teale, 1982). The vignette at the beginning of the chapter demonstrates both an explicit lesson and learning in a meaningful context. The teacher had taught explicit lessons that focused just on the phonics skill, and then she put that information into real-life contexts. Letter–sound instruction must build on a child's concept of the whole process of reading (Stahl, 1992). Phonics instruction helps children to recognize words quickly and automatically so they can turn their attention to comprehension of the text.

Effective phonics instruction includes sufficient practice in reading and writing words both in context and in isolation. The teacher needs to find the best mix of methods to meet students' needs. Administrators need to help teachers form study groups and provide professional development to help teachers with these issues.

Systematic phonics programs teach letter–sound relations in a specific sequence, although different authorities recommend different sequence patterns. The systematic teaching of phonics can take many different forms, such as the synthetic approach, which translates letter combinations into sounds and then blends these combinations into words; the analytic approach, which analyzes letter–sound relations in words the students already know; and the analogy-based approach, which uses word families or word parts to help students identify and recognize new words. Finally, the approach of teaching phonics through spelling separates words into phonemes first and then has students write the letters that correspond to the phonemes (Armbruster et al., 2001; Cunningham, 1999; Stahl, Duffy-Hester, & Stahl, 1998).

Synthetic phonics instruction teaches the sounds each letter makes before combining them to form words. For example, after the short *a* sound /a/ has been taught, along with the /b/, /t/, and /m/ sounds, students can begin pronouncing the words *bat, mat, tab,* and *bam.* After students learn enough sounds, they can begin to read easily decodable books containing a limited number of words. They also can write stories using the words they know. Teachers can use books containing some of the sounds students know in read-alouds.

Analytic phonics instruction begins with a word or word part that the student knows, breaks it into its component parts, and then builds from it. For example, the teacher can write the word *cat* on the board, noting the /a/ sound. The teacher then can write words such as *fat, mat, shout, brat,* and *eat* on the board, pronouncing each word. The students should be able to identify the words that have the same /a/ sound as *cat* (Stahl et al., 1998). Over time, the students will learn phonics rules and generalizations based on those words (Cunningham, 1999).

Analogy-based instruction can be taught successfully using both word families and other word-building activities. Analogy-based methods begin with a word or word part the child already knows and uses it to help identify other words containing the same part. For example, once the student has learned *park,* he or she should be able to read *dark* and *bark.* Students should begin to see the patterns in words and use those patterns to help them pronounce new words.

Teaching phonics through spelling is "based on students' developmental levels of orthographic knowledge" (Stahl et al., 1998, p. 346). Similar to analogy-based methods, the spelling instruction method relies on patterns and similar word parts. Word sorts (e.g., classifying all short vowel words together) and Making Words (Cunningham, 1999; see p. 37) are two activities that can help teach students about word parts and their spellings. What makes this strategy different from the analogy-based strategy is the focus on the letters and their corresponding sounds (phonemes) that compose the words.

According to Stahl (1992), there is a recommended sequence for teaching phonics. However, when teachable moments occur, teachers should take advantage of them whether or not they are within recommended sequences. Phonics instruction frequently begins with the most commonly used initial consonants sounds, such as /f/, /m/, /s/, /t/, and /h/, and then progresses to these same sounds in ending word positions. The next set of initial and final consonant sounds usually taught is /l/, /d/, /c/, /n/, /g/, /w/, /p/, /r/, /k/, then /j/, /q/, /v/, final /x/, blends, consonant digraphs, and finally some structural aspects of words. Vowel sounds are taught beginning with short vowels, then moving to long vowel sounds, vowel pairs, and so forth. Because students need to practice all of these skills, they should be reviewed frequently. Syllabication, contractions, prefixes, suffixes, synonyms, antonyms, and homonyms are then taught, as appropriate (Morrow, 2005).

The goal of phonics instruction is to help students learn and use the alphabetic principle—the understanding that there are systematic and predictable relations between written letters and spoken sounds. It is important that phonics instruction takes place within a meaningful context, along with some systematic and explicit teaching of skills. It is also important that students have continual practice to learn sound–symbol relations; rarely is a single lesson sufficient. Administrators should encourage teachers to provide ongoing experiences with letters and letter–sound combinations beyond the initial instruction and to continually review them with students as often as possible. In addition, administrators should provide professional development opportunities that concentrate on this aspect of teaching phonics.

Using Strategies to Teach Specific Concepts

When teaching phonics, teachers should include explicit instruction and meaningful contexts, as has already been mentioned. The need for both types of instruction is often difficult for both teachers and administrators to understand. The sample lessons that follow are provided as a means of clarifying this concept and are written in a way that will allow administrators to guide and support teachers in their endeavors to provide phonics instruction through both explicit instruction and meaningful contexts.

The sample lessons that follow begin with whole-class explicit instruction, then move to more guided practice, and finally end with some independent activities. When teaching about topics in the early primary grades, teachers should incorporate visual, auditory, olfactory, and tactile experiences—that is, experiences that include seeing, hearing, smelling, and touching.

Teaching Initial Consonant Sounds

Objective of the Lesson
Students will learn sound–symbol relations using initial consonants.

Materials
Storybooks, large surface for writing (chart on easel or blackboard), clipboard, journal or index cards, collage supplies such as tissue paper, foil, doilies, and wallpaper

Procedure

1. The teacher begins the literacy block with an introduction to the initial consonant p and asks students if they have the letter p in their names.

2. The teacher introduces the sound of the letter p, and the students make the sound along with her.

3. The teacher selects a book for a read-aloud that has many words in it with the initial consonant p. For example, teachers might select *The Pig's Picnic* (Kasza, 1988) because of its many initial consonant p words.

4. Before reading, the teacher shares the book's pictures with the students and some of the words that begin with the letter p. The teacher asks the students to listen carefully for two words that begin with the letter p as she reads the story.

5. After reading the story, the teacher asks the students which initial consonant p words they remember. She writes them on a chart as the students mention them.

6. The teacher asks the students to look through a picture storybook to find words that begin with p and then write them down in their journals or on index cards to read later.

Variations

Students go on a word hunt around the classroom looking for words with the initial consonant *p* and write them on a piece of paper attached to a clipboard.

Students create a collage of pictures that represent words with the initial consonant *p*.

The class creates a story using lots of words with the initial consonant *p* and dictates it to the teacher.

Blending Initial Consonants and Ending Word Families

Objective of the Lesson
Students will pronounce all of the sounds in a word after it is segmented and then blend initial consonants and ending word families together.

Materials
Classroom morning message, chalkboard, chart paper, laminated cards, magnetic letters of initial consonants and ending word families, paper

Procedure

1. The teacher tells the students they will be learning about the beginnings and endings of words. Beginning letters of words are called *initial consonants*, and the endings are called *word families*.

2. The teacher reads the morning message for content related to the class theme.

3. The teacher reads the morning message again, looking specifically at particular words for their initial consonants and word family endings.

4. The teacher puts the words from the morning message on chart paper to show the students how a word can be segmented into the initial consonant and word family, making sure to carefully pronounce each part. The teacher asks the students to repeat the parts and the word after him or her.

5. The teacher asks the whole class to make as many words as they can with word family endings such as *at*, *ar*, and *an*.

6. The teacher records all responses for the rest of the students to see on chart paper or on the chalkboard.

7. The teacher then introduces the Making Words activity by handing each student three to five initial consonant letters and ending word family cards to arrange. For example, the teacher could say, "Make the

word *cat*. Now take the *c* from *cat* and put a letter in front of it to make *hat*. Put the letter *b* in front of the *at* to make *bat*."

8. The teacher asks the students to create words using the words endings *at*, *ar*, and *an*.

9. The teacher provides the students with paper to write down the words they create.

Variations

Teachers can construct a board game in which students create words with initial consonants and word families in order to advance on the board. Then, students sort the words they created into three columns: those with the *at*, *ar*, and *an* endings.

Using Phonics and Context to Figure Out a Word

Objective of the Lesson

Students will use their knowledge of phonics and the meaning of a sentence to figure out an unknown word.

Materials

Morning message, chart paper or chalkboard, selected poems

Procedure

1. The teacher uses the morning message to show how people can figure out words by understanding what the sentence means and looking at the letters in the unknown word.

2. The teacher introduces the strategy called Guess the Covered Word (Cunningham, 1999) to help students use the context of a sentence to decode a word and the letters in the word. The teacher writes the morning message on chart paper or the chalkboard, covering up or leaving blanks for the target words or high-frequency words from the curriculum thematic words. For example, the teacher might write the following: Today, we will go outside to _____. When we watch the movie, we will eat _____.

3. The students predict the missing word from the context. Then, they look at the initial sound of the word to determine if their prediction is correct.

4. If a student's prediction is not correct based on the initial consonant sound and the meaning of the sentence, the teacher asks the students to make another prediction.

Variation

Students figure out the missing word within a poem written on a chart prepared by the teacher.

Additional General Strategies

Additional general activities that can be used to practice any phonics skill include the following:

- The teacher, students, or both can collect items that begin with a particular sound and place them in sound boxes, or boxes labeled with a designated letter.
- The teacher can collect sensory articles for a letter. For example, for the letter *p*, the teacher can collect items such as Puppy Chow dog food to smell, popcorn to eat, peacock plumes to touch, a purring cat sound to listen to, and a book to look at that contains a lot of *p* words.
- Students can collect their Very Own Words with phonics elements such as initial consonants, blends, long and short vowels, and so forth. Words can be written on index cards and stored in plastic baggies.
- The teacher, students, or both can make up short stories that emphasize a sound, such as the following for the letter *p*:
  My name is Penelope Pig.
  I pick petals from petunias.
  I play patty-cake
  And eat pretzels with pink punch.
- Students can make a writing journal in which they note the phonic elements they learn.
- The teacher and students can make class books emphasizing different phonic elements.

For teachers to use these activities with students, there are certain materials the teachers need in their classrooms. Classrooms need to be outfitted with basic materials for practicing phonics skills. Teachers need to create a word wall for practicing phonics, and they need to help students practice phonics skills using board games, such as matching games, memory games, phonics bingo, and puzzle games. Teachers need sets of magnetic, cardboard, and sponge letters along with sets of letter chunks for building words. Then, teachers and students can build words on magnetic boards, white boards, and in pocket charts.

Administrators should be cognizant of these needs and appropriate funds accordingly.

Conclusion

Early literacy educators have often had concerns about teaching phonics. They question exactly what skills should be taught, when to introduce them, how to teach them, and how much time to spend dealing with them. Although there are no definitive answers to all these questions, dialogue among teachers and administrators can provide insight into ways to address them. Currently research has found that teaching phonics by using a variety of approaches seems to work best. For example, there should be some explicit, systematic instruction; spontaneous instruction; and opportunities to practice skills both with guidance and independently. In addition, instruction should be placed in meaningful contexts as often as possible.

When teaching sound–symbol relations, teachers need to be aware of dialects. If a teacher from New York taught in the southern part of United States, he or she would teach long and short vowels with different sounds than those taught by a teacher who was from the South. Students in most parts of the United States live in communities composed of children who speak many different dialects and attend the same school. These children may have difficulty dealing with sounds, regardless of where their teacher is from (Morrow, 2005).

Students learn new material when it is repeated and practiced. They also learn as a result of being exposed to material in different modalities; for example, using visual clues, auditory clues, sensory experiences, and tactile experiences. Teaching the same phonic skills in many different ways provides all children with the opportunity to learn the skill in the modality that best suits them. Administrators who are knowledgeable about the need for effective phonics instruction as well as reliable strategies for teaching it can alleviate many of the concerns held by early literacy educators. By working together, administrators and teachers can develop the phonics program that best meets the needs of the school and its students.

REFERENCES

Armbruster, B.B., Lehr, F., & Osborn, J. (2001). *Put reading first: The research building blocks for teaching children to read.* Washington, DC: Partnership for Reading.

Cunningham, P.M. (1999). What should we do about phonics? In L.B. Gambrell, L.M. Morrow, S.B. Neuman, & M. Pressley (Eds.), *Best practices in literacy instruction* (pp. 68–89). New York: Guilford.

Morrow, L.M. (2005). *Literacy development in the early years: Helping children read and write* (5th ed.). Boston: Allyn & Bacon.

Morrow, L.M., & Tracey, D.H. (1997). Strategies used for phonics instruction in early childhood classrooms. *The Reading Teacher, 50*(8), 644–651.

National Institute of Child Health and Human Development. (2000). *Report of the National Reading Panel. Teaching children to read: An evidence-based assessment of the scientific research literature on reading and its implications for reading instruction* (NIH Publication No. 00-4769). Washington, DC: U.S. Government Printing Office.

No Child Left Behind Act of 2001, Pub. L. No. 107-110, 115 Stat. 1425 (2002). Retrieved October 1, 2005, from http://edworkforce.house.gov/issues/107th/education/nclb/nclb.htm

Stahl, S.A. (1992). Saying the "p" word: Nine guidelines for exemplary phonics instruction. *The Reading Teacher, 45*(8), 618–625.

Stahl, S.A., Duffy-Hester, A., & Stahl, K. (1998). Everything you wanted to know about phonics (but were afraid to ask). *Reading Research Quarterly, 33*(3), 338–355.

Teale, W.H. (1982). Toward a theory of how children learn to read and write naturally. *Language Arts, 59*(6), 555–570.

LITERATURE CITED

Brett, J. (1994). *Town mouse and country mouse*. New York: Puffin.

Kasza, K. (1988). *The pig's picnic*. New York: Putnam.

CHAPTER 4

Vocabulary Instruction: New Ideas and Time-Tested Strategies

James Flood, Diane Lapp, and Sharon Flood

AS MS. KELLY MOORE, a kindergarten and first-grade teacher, calls her students to the carpet to teach them about weather, she realizes (once more) that they have never experienced snow. Most of her students are Mexican Americans who have spent their entire lives in Mexico or San Diego. As part of her previous lesson on weather, she discussed precipitation and various types of rainfall.

Today, she continues her conversation with her students about precipitation by looking at snow forms. She shows them pictures of snow falling on leaves, children frolicking in the snow, giant snowmen, and perfectly formed snowballs. She carefully explains that snowstorms can be quite severe and even dangerous before she begins reading *Blizzard* (Murphy, 2000), an illustrated trade book about the blizzard of 1888. The children are enthralled, and together with Ms. Moore, they decide to draw snow scenes to display together with the book jacket from *Blizzard* on their literature board.

Angelica, a wide-eyed, alert 6-year-old is very excited as she draws her picture. When Ms. Moore asks if she wants to write a sentence beneath her drawing, Angelica enthusiastically says, "Yes." She enhances her picture of a car with snow all over it and a particularly big pile on the hood with her sentence, "I liked the part about when the man opened the door and saw a blizzard on his car."

Understanding and Implementing Reading First Initiatives: The Changing Role of Administrators by Carrice Cummins, Editor. Copyright © 2006 by the International Reading Association.
Classroom examples and figures in this chapter are adapted from Brassell, D., & Flood, J. (2004). *Vocabulary strategies every teacher should know*. San Diego, CA: Academic Professional Development.

Ms. Moore smiles, helps Angelica with her writing, and thinks to herself, "In time, with more practice and many more exposures to the nuances of this word, Angelica will really own this word. For now, she's learned what she needed about blizzards to get started."

Angelica was provided with excellent instruction from Ms. Moore through the use of realia (e.g., pictures), conversation, drawing, writing, and questioning. Yet Angelica only learned some of what she would need to know to generalize from her experience of the word *blizzard* to other blizzards. Angelica is in the first stage of her word learning about the concept of a blizzard. Neither her experiences as a Southern Californian nor her experiences with the book *Blizzard* and Ms. Moore's explanation provided enough background schema for her to fully understand this word. What she needs, and what Ms. Moore will give her, is more time with this concept through multiple exposures to the word in a variety of instructional contexts.

The importance of vocabulary instruction sits prominently on the list of essential components of reading instruction identified by the No Child Left Behind Act (NCLB) of 2001 and the National Reading Panel Report of 2000 (National Institute of Child Health and Human Development [NICHD]). Therefore, all school administrators, language arts supervisors, and literacy coaches need to know everything they can about effective vocabulary instruction to ensure that all students are given ample opportunities to understand the words in their in-school and out-of-school environments.

Consequently, in this chapter we present administrators with new ideas and time-tested strategies in the area of teaching vocabulary—each with a strong research base. We believe that administrators can provide the first line of knowledge in every school; they need to establish the climate that fosters growth in children in every school. Principals and other administrators make the difference between schools that work well and schools that need help.

We begin with an overview of what is known about effective vocabulary instruction, and then we offer examples of good practices. By looking inside classrooms in which excellent teachers are teaching their children new words every day, administrators can get a glimpse of extraordinary practices that they can help to export to their own schools.

Defining Vocabulary Instruction

Vocabulary knowledge, arguably one of the most important hallmarks of an educated person, is essential for comprehending texts at all levels. It plays a vital role in every aspect of reading, from understanding the plot or gist of a simple text to interpreting and appreciating the most complex texts (Beck, McKeown, & Kucan, 2002; Brassell & Flood, 2004; Lapp, Flood, Brock, & Fisher, in press; Nagy & Anderson, 1984).

Vocabulary knowledge among various populations of school-aged children in the United States has become alarming dichotomous in recent years. Graves and Slater (1987) reported that first graders from middle class and affluent families know twice as many words as children from families living in poverty. These data, coupled with Biemiller's (1999) and Hart and Risley's (1995) findings that the differences between middle- and upper-class children and their lower class counterparts were virtually insurmountable in the current educational culture, are particularly disturbing.

However, what initially appeared to be a grim finding from the research on vocabulary instruction in schools—the absence of explicit instruction in vocabulary in most classrooms (Biemiller, 2001; Scott, Jamieson-Noel, & Asselin, 2003)—actually offers educators a unique opportunity to change the course of children's lives by directly teaching vocabulary. Several studies indicate that children from all social classes can be taught vocabulary when the instruction is robust and explicit (for a detailed review of robust vocabulary teaching, see Beck et al., 2002; Brassell & Flood, 2004).

In this chapter, we examine the ways in which robust, explicit vocabulary instruction can be offered in classrooms at all age levels. Before presenting specific instructional strategies that administrators can share with teachers, we discuss the major contemporary issues in vocabulary teaching—that is, what words to teach, what criteria to use for selecting words, and the best ways to teach vocabulary to elementary-grade children.

Learning New Vocabulary Through Oral and Print Exposure

Young children and beginning readers develop their vocabulary knowledge through oral language exchanges, while older students (approximately ages 7 and beyond) who have advanced beyond the earliest stages of reading learn most of their new vocabulary words through experiences with print (Carnine, Kame'enui, & Coyle, 1984; Elley, 1989).

When young children begin reading books on their own, the words in the text have to be carefully chosen to account for children's developing decoding skills. Beginning texts often include sentences such as these: "Matt likes food. Matt likes pizza. Pizza is good." These brief, simple sentences are supported with rich illustrations to enable children to comprehend written texts as they begin their journey into becoming independent, literate adults.

These texts for beginning readers are, by necessity, limited in the types of vocabulary words they include, and most such texts contain few new or unfamiliar vocabulary concepts. The vocabulary instruction that occurs with these easy and familiar words is delivered orally in most cases because there are so few words in the text that require teaching for meaning. To help children acquire a set of new words, teachers typically introduce new words through their conversations about the words in the text. For example, in one classroom we observed a teacher using her conversation time to help children learn new vocabulary words. After she charted the children's favorite foods, the teacher placed the food words into a simple sentence (e.g., Pizza tastes good, Candy tastes good, Cake tastes good). The teacher then turned to a new page on her easel board and asked the children to brainstorm new words that could be used to say "good." The chart was quickly filled with printed words such as *delicious*, *yummy*, and *scrumptious*. Each time the children reread the text, they asked if they could substitute one of their new words when they came to the sentence "Pizza is good." Although only a few of the children were initially able to decode (or encode) *scrumptious* and *delicious*, they were adding these words to their oral language repertoires.

Throughout the rest of their lives, however, the bulk of these and other children's new vocabulary words will be learned from print. Cunningham and Stanovich (1998) have shown that even highly educated adults rarely use unfamiliar words in their informal conversations—17.3 rare words per 1,000 words and only 28 rare words per 1,000 in their oral technical presentations. By contrast, schoolbooks contain almost twice as many new words per 1,000 (i.e., 52.7).

For children to begin learning new vocabulary through exposure to print, they need wide exposure to print in many genres and formats. The adage "the more you read, the stronger your vocabulary will become" has been frequently demonstrated in vocabulary research studies, including those that explicitly show the link between vocabulary knowledge and reading comprehension ability. (For a review of the research studies, see Beck et al., 2002.)

The Four Questions Teachers Most Frequently Ask About Vocabulary Instruction

The following questions represent some of the most frequent questions that teachers ask about vocabulary instruction:

1. How many words can I teach in one year? In one lesson?

2. What words should I teach?

3. How many encounters or exposures are necessary before a student "owns" a new vocabulary word?

4. How can I effectively teach vocabulary?

In the following sections, we provide answers that may prove helpful to administrators as they assist teachers in implementing effective vocabulary instruction.

How Many Words Can I Teach in One Year? In One Lesson?

While estimates vary, the easy answer to how many words a teacher can teach students is about 400 per year. Beck et al. (2002) concluded that 400 words per year was a reasonable estimate of the number of words that could be taught and learned by children of all ages in one school year based on the following assumptions: (a) There are approximately 88,000 word families in English (e.g., view, preview, review, previewing, viewed; Nagy & Anderson, 1984); (b) more than half of these words are so rare that most people will only encounter them once in their lives, if at all; (c) children already know about 8,000 common words; and (d) there are about 7,000 new, unknown words that occur frequently in school texts. If these 7,000 words are divided among grades K through 9, that leaves each grade with 700 words per year, which is probably an unreasonable stretch for teachers and students. Therefore, Beck and her associates (2002) decided to try to teach a little more than half that number, 400 words per year, and they had a great deal of success in their studies.

If approximately 400 words can be taught per year, about how many words should be taught in one lesson? Again, there is an easy answer: five new, unfamiliar words per lesson. When teachers try to extend this number by pulling out and preteaching all of the difficult words that children will encounter in a new text (and the list grows to 10–20 words), they are courting disaster. For each new word introduced beyond five, a teacher can count on memory overload, which negatively affects the learning of the five target words.

However, a caveat is needed here. First, not all children know the same words, so some of the words that teachers choose as new words will not be new for every child. Second, introducing new words through known words enables teachers to introduce many more than five new words at a time (a concept that will be discussed in more detail later in the chapter).

What Words Should I Teach?

Anyone who has stopped to ponder this question has been immediately overwhelmed by the myriad of choices: (1) content-area words (words usually associated with specific subjects) such as *constitution, republic, declaration, amendment,* and *emancipation;* (2) grade-level high-frequency words; (3) high-utility (but lower frequency) words such as *imaginative, design, adjustable,* and *creative;* and (4) literary words such as *symbolism, image, plot,* and *characterization.* Although the list of possibilities seems endless, as educators we have to make some sensible choices that are based on sound criteria.

Criteria for Selecting Vocabulary Words to Be Taught. In an attempt to determine the words that should be taught, Graves (2000), building on the early work of Dale, O'Rourke, and Bamman (1971), advises teachers to make a distinction between teaching new concepts and teaching new labels for familiar concepts. Laufer and Nation (1999) add that dividing words into four very useful categories is helpful:

1. high-frequency words (e.g., *car, driver*)
2. domain-specific technical vocabulary (e.g., *raceway*)
3. low-frequency words (e.g., *carburetor*)
4. high-utility words (e.g., *gasoline*)

Beck and her colleagues (2002) provide a third framework for categorizing words into three tiers: Tier I words, which consist of words that are almost universally known (e.g., *mom, happy,* and *sad*); Tier II words, which include almost all of the words we need to teach students; and Tier III words, which are infrequent and technical (e.g., *photosynthesis* and *hubris*) and are best learned at their point of need.

A sensible set of criteria for selecting Tier II words includes the following:

- Choose words that have high utility in students' lives.
- Choose words that will lead students to other words.
- Choose words that are needed in a particular content area.

How Many Encounters or Exposures to Words Are Needed?

Some researchers (Beck et al., 2002; Miller, 1978; Nagy & Scott, 2000) have suggested that it takes at least 8 to 10 exposures to a new word for it to begin to become part of a child's lexicon. Although it is obvious that the real answer to this question depends on the child's background as well as the word itself, it seems clear that words do take time "to own." As Vygotsky (1934/1986), Cronbach (1942), Dale (1965), Calfee and Drum (1986), and Brassell and Flood (2004) note, vocabulary development is incremental—that is, we never really own most words; we just grow in our understanding of the concepts they represent.

How Can I Effectively Teach Vocabulary?

There is no one best way to teach vocabulary to every child. Children learn word meanings in multiple ways, ranging from learning words incidentally (e.g., from read-alouds) to learning words from robust, explicit, and effective instruction from their teachers.

Read-Alouds. Children learn words incidentally from texts that are read to them. In one kindergarten classroom, for example, we observed that children learned the word *mischief* from Sendak's *Where the Wild Things Are* (1963) as their teacher read the book to them. The book opens with the sentence "The night Max made mischief of one kind or another" and is illustrated with a picture of Max riding a banister in his home. When the teacher queried the students on the meaning of the word *mischief*, they all had a rudimentary knowledge of its meaning. They certainly did not have a sophisticated grasp of the word—that requires many more exposures to the word—but they had grasped a beginning-level knowledge of the word.

Robust, Explicit, and Effective Instruction. Children also learn words directly from robust, direct, and explicit instruction. Regardless of whether the learning is incidental from indirect teaching or direct from explicit teacher instruction, children have to situate their words within their own lexicons—that is, they have to learn new words in relation to the words they already know. They have to learn words in a conceptual network based on the theory that every newly learned word is related to other already known words (Nagy, 1988). Children not only have to understand the meaning of the new word, but they also have to understand how words are related to one another.

Instructional Strategies

Several effective instructional strategies can be used to help children build important conceptual networks. Using instructional strategies to teach vocabulary has many positive elements—strategies introduce new words and ideas in a systematic manner that helps children learn through modeling and practice—but these strategies also have a potential downside: They can be overtaught. Once a child has acquired a strategy, it is not necessary to continue teaching that strategy.

What is needed, however, is direct instruction in helping children know which strategy to use, how to use it, and when to use it. In the following sections, we introduce several vocabulary strategies that are situated in actual classrooms to demonstrate the ways in which each strategy helps the teacher meet the students' needs.

There are many different ways in which effective strategies can be classified. For the purposes of this chapter, we will classify these strategies into three broad categories: (1) visual display strategies, (2) discussion and conversation strategies, and (3) performance strategies. Although these categories overlap to some extent, they help to illustrate the underlying cognitive and linguistic processes that make the strategies effective.

Visual Display Strategies

Teachers can use a number of different visual strategies to help children "see" the relations among the target word and other words related to it. Some of these key strategies include using semantic maps, conceptual ladders, semantic feature analysis grids, and hierarchical array charts.

Semantic Maps. Semantic maps are particularly useful for visually representing new word meanings and the relation between the new word and other known words. Semantic mapping (Blachowicz & Johnson, 1994; Heimlich & Pittleman, 1986; Pittleman, Heimlich, Berglund, & French, 1991), also known as semantic webbing and semantic networking, often includes the use of a graphic organizer resembling a spider web to organize information by categories.

In the following example, semantic mapping is used to show how children learned words associated with the focus word *dinosaur*. The teacher teaches the children about the word *dinosaur*, which is a Tier I word for most children. It is not a new concept; therefore, it does not count as one of the 400 words for the year. It may be a new *written* word for many children, but it is probably not an unknown word. In this lesson, *dinosaur* is the focus word that leads to three new words that the teacher wants to teach—(1) *extinct*, (2) *survival*, and (3) *fossil*. The words linking *dinosaur* with the target words are all Tier I words (e.g., *lived*, *earth*, *water*, and *land*); they keep the network operating. The linking words *lived* and *became* are critical for understanding the relations among the words that are included in the semantic map (see Figure 4.1). They serve as review words that help children place the new words in a functioning network.

Rogelio Martinez's second graders are beginning a unit on dinosaurs. He wants his students to understand how scientists could prove dinosaurs' existence and why the dinosaurs became extinct. Mr. Martinez writes the word *dinosaurs* on

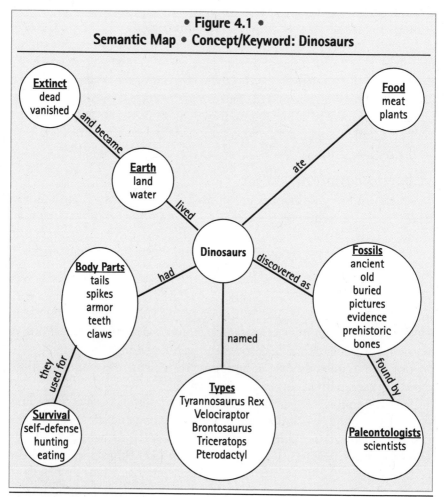

• Figure 4.1 •
Semantic Map • Concept/Keyword: Dinosaurs

Adapted from Brassell, D., & Flood, J. (2004). *Vocabulary strategies every teacher should know*. San Diego, CA: Academic Professional Development.

the chalkboard and asks students to organize into groups of three or four. Next, he asks the groups to brainstorm among themselves words that are associated with dinosaurs. He tells the groups to pay attention to characteristics the words share so they can categorize them under subheadings. After about five minutes, Mr. Martinez asks the groups to dictate the words they came up with while he writes them on the chalkboard. Students are encouraged to place words under categories. For example, when students share the words *ancient* and *old*, Mr. Martinez explains that dinosaur remains are also known as *fossils* and he places the terms under that category. Later, when students say that dinosaurs lived on *land* and in *water*, a student suggests that Mr. Martinez categorize those terms under *Earth*. After further discussion, students ask Mr. Martinez to connect categories with the key word *dinosaur* by writing relationship words on the connecting lines. For example, one student asks Mr. Martinez to connect *dinosaurs* and *food* with the word *ate*. Finally, Mr. Martinez tells students to add words and categories to the semantic map as they learn more about dinosaurs.

Concept Ladders. Concept ladders are designed to help students focus on a particular word or concept, rather than on a set or list of words. The new word or concept appears in the center of the ladder, and the students "climb up" the ladder to determine what the word or concept is and what it is composed of or "climb down" the ladder to determine examples and uses of the word or concept. Figure 4.2 illustrates how the concept word *narrative* might be developed.

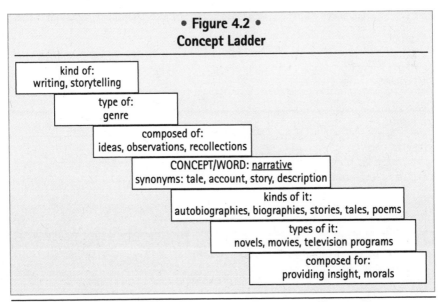

• Figure 4.2 •
Concept Ladder

kind of:
writing, storytelling

type of:
genre

composed of:
ideas, observations, recollections

CONCEPT/WORD: narrative
synonyms: tale, account, story, description

kinds of it:
autobiographies, biographies, stories, tales, poems

types of it:
novels, movies, television programs

composed for:
providing insight, morals

Adapted from Brassell, D., & Flood, J. (2004). *Vocabulary strategies every teacher should know.* San Diego, CA: Academic Professional Development.

Semantic Feature Analysis Grids. Semantic feature analysis is used to help students understand relations between words. Figure 4.3 shows a completed semantic feature analysis grid in which the differences among the words *valleys, mountains, coastline, deserts, forests,* and *swamps* are identified visually.

Hierarchical Array Charts. Hierarchical array charts also help students develop an understanding of relations between words. Figure 4.4 shows a completed chart of a unit of study on the scientific method.

Discussion and Conversation Strategies

Vocabulary instruction that actively involves students in dialogic conversations with one another helps them construct meaning that goes beyond what they could construct alone. Discussion and conversation strategies such as K-W-L Plus and scavenger hunts allow students to work together to develop conceptual understanding. K-W-L Plus (Ogle, 1986, 1992) is

• Figure 4.3 •
Semantic Feature Analysis Grid

	Heavily Populated	Soil Used for Farming	Developed	Hot	Wildlife	Boats Used for Transport	Tornadoes	Little Water
Valleys/ prairies	+	+	+	+	+	–	+	?
Mountains	–	–	?	–	+	–	–	–
Coastline (beaches)	+	–	+	?	+	+	–	–
Deserts	–	–	–	+	+	–	–	+
Forests	–	+	–	–	+	+	–	–
Swamps/ wetlands	–	–	–	?	+	+	–	–

Concept: Geographic Regions of the United States
+ = Students believe feature is true of that region.
– = Students believe region lacks that feature.
? = Students disagree whether region matches feature; students will seek answer in their reading.

Adapted from Brassell, D., & Flood, J. (2004). *Vocabulary strategies every teacher should know*. San Diego, CA: Academic Professional Development.

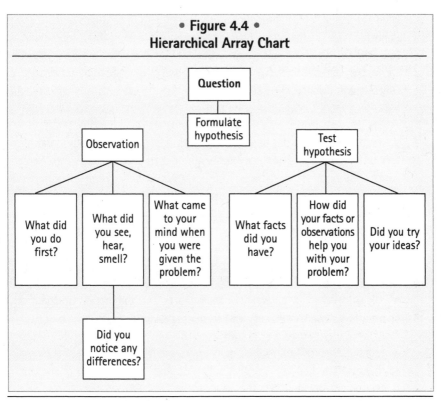

• Figure 4.4 •
Hierarchical Array Chart

Question

Formulate hypothesis

Observation

Test hypothesis

What did you do first?

What did you see, hear, smell?

What came to your mind when you were given the problem?

What facts did you have?

How did your facts or observations help you with your problem?

Did you try your ideas?

Did you notice any differences?

Adapted from Brassell, D., & Flood, J. (2004). *Vocabulary strategies every teacher should know*. San Diego, CA: Academic Professional Development.

an instructional strategy that uses conversation and discussion as its underlying principle; it enables children to assume an active role before, during, and after reading. It requires students to focus on four questions, two before they read and two after they read: What I know (K), What I want to learn (W), What I learned (L), and What I still need to learn (+). K-W-L Plus focuses on the meanings of words as well as the meanings of whole passages. This strategy is used to engage students' interest by making them active participants in their reading; allow students to brainstorm and categorize their ideas prior to reading informational text; clarify to students the purpose(s) of their reading; and encourage students to constantly ask themselves questions before, during, and after their reading.

Maria Vasquez's third graders are learning about important U.S. landmarks, symbols, and essential documents. She shows her students a book of photographs of various U.S. landmarks and asks students if they recognize any. A few days later, Ms. Vasquez tells students that they are going to continue to learn about important U.S. landmarks and symbols by reading a book about Independence Day—the Fourth of July—and learning why U.S. citizens celebrate this day. She shows her class the book *Fireworks, Picnics, and Flags: The Story of the Fourth of July Symbols* (Giblin, 2001) and asks students if they can identify various symbols on the book's cover (e.g., the American flag and the Statue of Liberty).

Ms. Vasquez distributes K-W-L Plus strategy charts to the class and asks students to brainstorm what they know about Independence Day. Students volunteer different information they know about the Fourth of July, and then the entire class describes ways they could classify their information into categories: what we know, what we want to know, what we learned, and what we still want to learn. Ms. Vasquez asks student volunteers to share some of their information. She writes their responses on the chalkboard in the "K" column of her chart. After naming six categories, the class looks at the list of things they know and they place each piece of information into one of the categories. Ms. Vasquez asks each student to write down questions they have about the Fourth of July under the "W" category of their charts, and she models on the chalkboard a few sample questions that students provide.

After students read a selection from the book, Ms. Vasquez asks them to write down the answers to their questions under the "L" column of their strategy sheets. She then asks for student volunteers to share some of the things they learned from their reading, and she writes their responses on the chalkboard K-W-L Plus chart. Finally, Ms. Vasquez asks the class to share some of the new questions they had regarding Independence Day. She lists students' questions on the chalkboard under the "+" column and asks students to write their own questions on their strategy sheets. She asks students where they might find the answers to their questions and tells them they will continue studying more about important U.S. landmarks, symbols, and essential documents throughout the week. (See Figure 4.5 for the complete K-W-L Plus sheet that Ms. Vasquez's class generated.)

Another example of a discussion and conversation strategy is a scavenger hunt, an instructional activity that enhances students' vocabulary through conversations they have as they work together to gather objects and pictures representing concepts that need to be more fully developed (Cunningham, Moore, Cunningham, & Moore, 1995). For example, a third-grade class that had just finished reading *Millions to Measure* (Schwartz, 2000) was preparing to study weights and measures. Their teacher, Mrs. Lungren, had selected 10 words (*ruler, thermometer, scale, clock, degrees, gallon, weight, centimeter, temperature,* and *miles*) from the book and other books that the students would be reading

• Figure 4.5 •
K–W–L Plus: Independence Day

K What We Know	W What We Want to Know	L What We Learned	+ What We Still Need to Learn

(5) fireworks
(2) apple pie
(2) hot dogs
(2) Liberty Bell
(1) Independence
    Hall
(1, 2) Statue of
    Liberty
(3) Declaration of
    Independence
(4) Benjamin
    Franklin
(4) George
    Washington
(4) Thomas
    Jefferson
(1) White House
(5) parades
(2) American flag
(3) National
    Anthem
(6) Fourth of July
	Why do we
	celebrate
	Independence Day?
	
	Why is
	Independence Day
	on July 4th?
	
	Why is Benjamin
	Franklin on $100
	bills?
	
	What is the
	Declaration of
	Independence?
	
	Why do we have
	fireworks on
	Independence Day?
		Thomas Jefferson
		wrote the
		Declaration of
		Independence.
		
		The Declaration of
		Independence made
		America
		independent from
		the British.
		
		The Declaration of
		Independence was
		passed on July 4,
		1776, in
		Philadelphia in
		Independence Hall.
		
		Benjamin Franklin,
		Thomas Jefferson,
		and many others
		signed the
		Declaration of
		Independence.
			Why is Benjamin
			Franklin on $100
			bills?
			
			Why did Benjamin
			Franklin never
			become President?
			
			Why did the first
			American flag only
			have 13 stars?
			
			Why did we keep
			fighting the British
			after we signed the
			Declaration of
			Independence?
			
			Does any other
			country have a
			Declaration of
			Independence?
			
			Why was the
			Declaration of
			Independence signed
			in Philadelphia, not
			Washington, DC?

Categories of Information We Expect to See:
(1) landmark
(2) symbol
(3) essential document
(4) historical figure
(5) celebration activity
(6) important date

Note: Ms. Vasquez asked students to categorize the information they knew associated with Independence Day. She numbered the categories that the class provided and wrote the number of the appropriate category to the left of each piece of information that students had listed in the "K" section of their chart. The "K" section represents the key vocabulary words the class would be using as they discussed Independence Day.

Adapted from Brassell, D., & Flood, J. (2004). *Vocabulary strategies every teacher should know.* San Diego, CA: Academic Professional Development.

about different forms of measurement. She gave the list to the students and explained that they needed to collect pictures and objects that illustrated each word. She provided class time for students to hunt through magazines. She also encouraged them to look for other objects and pictures at home and outside the classroom. Throughout the week, students conversed in groups about the objects and pictures they had found. At the end of the week, each group presented the "measurable memorabilia" they had collected. Through this activity, students' knowledge of weights and measures and their topical language were developed as they collected and conversed about their collections.

Performance Strategies

Performance strategies require students to enact the meaning of new words through dramatic interpretations. Word Play (Blachowicz & Fisher, 2002; Duffelmeyer, 1980) is an instructional strategy that utilizes dramatization to encourage students' vocabulary development. Using a short list of new vocabulary words or concepts, small groups of students create vignettes that feature and demonstrate the new vocabulary words or concepts. This strategy is used to motivate students to make predictions about the possible use of words in a new text, allow students to experiment with using words in their own speech, and provide students with the opportunity to collaborate and discuss various meanings of new vocabulary words and concepts. For example, during African American/ Black History Month a third-grade teacher invited his students to create short skits based on the vocabulary from Martin Luther King, Jr.'s historic "I Have A Dream" speech. The vocabulary list included words such as *Negro, discrimination, civil rights, destiny,* and *brotherhood.* Students read the speech and highlighted the new vocabulary. In small groups, they created their scripts, performed them for the group, and then discussed the similarities and differences between the text and their skits.

Conclusion

Teachers who provide students with many different reading materials and opportunities to read are off to a great start. In addition to wide reading, however, there are a number of strategies that teachers may use to facilitate vocabulary instruction. Just as students do not always respond to a particular book, not all students respond to a particular vocabulary strategy; therefore, it is important to know and implement many different strategies.

And as Rupley, Logan, and Nichols (1998) point out,

[T]eaching vocabulary versus incidental learning of words through wide reading should not be viewed as competing philosophies...vocabulary instruction that is geared to the active process of learning and connects new information to previously learned experiences provides the means for students to make the connection between new words and their past experiences. (p. 346)

Although the strategies presented in this chapter focus on visual displays, discussions and conversations, and performances, there are many other strategies that teachers have used to help their students learn new words. The strategies presented in this chapter offer a glimpse into the many ways that vocabulary can be taught and learned.

As one of the keys to literacy (NCLB, 2002; NICHD, 2000), vocabulary instruction is a complex phenomenon. Vocabulary growth is a life-long process, not a one-day activity. A comprehensive vocabulary program builds on the cognitive and linguistic foundations that underlie all effective teaching and learning approaches. Administrators need to ensure that schoolwide vocabulary programs are established so every child keeps learning new words and concepts. To guarantee that this happens, administrators need to stay current in the world of vocabulary. Just as words are living entities so, too, is vocabulary instruction. It is imperative that all administrators stay attuned to all of the new reliable research that will drive new and innovative practices.

REFERENCES

Beck, I.L., McKeown, M.G., & Kucan, L. (2002). *Bringing words to life: Robust vocabulary instruction*. New York: Guilford.

Biemiller, A. (1999, April). *Estimating vocabulary growth for ESL children with and without listening comprehension instruction*. Paper presented at the annual conference of the American Educational Research Association, Montréal, Québec, Canada.

Biemiller, A. (2001). Teaching vocabulary: Early, direct, and sequential. *American Educator, 25*(1), 24–28, 47.

Blachowicz, C.L.Z., & Fisher, P.J. (2002). *Teaching vocabulary in all classrooms* (2nd ed.). Upper Saddle River, NJ: Merrill/Prentice Hall.

Blachowicz, C.L.Z., & Johnson, B.E. (1994). Semantic mapping. In A.C. Purves (Ed.), *Encyclopedia of English studies in language arts* (pp. 116–127). New York: Scholastic.

Brassell, D., & Flood, J. (2004). *Vocabulary strategies every teacher should know*. San Diego, CA: Academic Professional Development.

Calfee, R.C., & Drum, P.A. (1986). Research on teaching reading. In M.C. Wittrock (Ed.), *Handbook of research on teaching* (3rd ed., pp. 804–849). New York: Macmillan.

Carnine, D.W., Kame'enui, E.J., & Coyle, G. (1984). Utilization of contextual information in determining the meaning of unfamiliar words. *Reading Research Quarterly, 19*(2), 188–204.

Cronbach, L.J. (1942). An analysis of techniques for diagnostic vocabulary testing. *Journal of Educational Research, 36*(3), 206–217.

Cunningham, A.E., & Stanovich, K.E. (1998). What reading does for the mind. *American Educator, 22*(1–2), 8–15.

Cunningham, P.M., Moore, S.A., Cunningham, J.W., & Moore, D.W. (1995). *Reading and writing in elementary classrooms: Strategies and observations* (3rd ed.). New York: Longman.

Dale, E. (1965). Vocabulary measurement: Techniques and major findings. *Elementary English, 42*, 82–88.

Dale, E., O'Rourke, J., & Bamman, H.A. (1971). *Techniques of teaching vocabulary.* Palo Alto, CA: Field Educational Publications.

Duffelmeyer, F.A. (1980). The influence of experience-based vocabulary instruction on learning word meanings. *Journal of Reading, 24*(1), 35–40.

Elley, W.B. (1989). Vocabulary acquisition from listening to stories. *Reading Research Quarterly, 24*(2), 174–187.

Graves, M. (2000). A vocabulary program to complement and bolster a middle-grade comprehension program. In B. Taylor, M. Graves, & P. van den Broek (Eds.), *Reading for meaning: Fostering comprehension in the middle grades* (pp. 116–135). New York: Teachers College Press.

Graves, M.F., & Slater, M.H. (1987, April). *The development of reading vocabularies of rural disadvantaged students, inner-city disadvantaged students, and middle-class suburban students.* Paper presented at the meeting of the American Educational Research Association, Washington, DC.

Hart, B., & Risley, T.R. (1995). *Meaningful differences in the everyday experience of young American children.* Baltimore: Brookes.

Heimlich, J.E., & Pittleman, S.D. (1986). *Semantic mapping: Classroom applications.* Newark, DE: International Reading Association.

Lapp, D., Flood, J., Brock, C., & Fisher, D. (in press). *Teaching reading to every child* (4th ed.). Mahwah, NJ: Erlbaum.

Laufer, B., & Nation, P. (1999). A vocabulary-size test of controlled productive ability. *Language Testing, 16*(1), 33–51.

Miller, G.A. (1978). Semantic relations among words. In M. Halle, J. Bresnan, & G.A. Miller (Eds.), *Linguistic theory and psychological reality* (pp. 61–118). Cambridge, MA: The MIT Press.

Nagy, W.E. (1988). *Teaching vocabulary to improve reading comprehension.* New York: National Council of Teachers of English; Newark, DE: International Reading Association.

Nagy, W.E., & Anderson, R.C. (1984). How many words are there in printed school English? *Reading Research Quarterly, 19*(3), 304–330.

Nagy, W.E., & Scott, J.A. (2000). Vocabulary processes. In M.L. Kamil, P.B. Mosenthal, P.D. Pearson, & R. Barr (Eds.), *Handbook of reading research* (Vol. 3, pp. 69–284). Mahwah, NJ: Erlbaum.

National Institute of Child Health and Human Development (NICHD). (2000). *Report of the National Reading Panel. Teaching children to read: An evidence-based assessment of the scientific research literature on reading and its implications for reading instruction* (NIH Publication No. 00-4769). Washington, DC: U.S. Government Printing Office.

No Child Left Behind Act of 2001, Pub. L. No. 107-110, 115 Stat. 1425 (2002). Retrieved October 1, 2005, from http://edworkforce.house.gov/issues/107th/education/nclb/nclb.htm

Ogle, D. (1986). K-W-L group instruction strategy. In A.S. Palincsar, D. Ogle, B.F. Jones, & E.G. Carr (Eds.), *Teaching reading as thinking*. Alexandria, VA: Association for Supervision and Curriculum Development.

Ogle, D. (1992). KWL in action: Secondary teachers find applications that work. In E.K. Dishner, T.W. Bean, J.E. Readence, & D.W. Moore (Eds.), *Reading in the content areas: Improving classroom instruction* (3rd ed.). Dubuque, IA: Kendall/Hunt.

Pittleman, S.D., Heimlich, J.E., Berglund, R.L., & French, M.P. (1991). *Semantic feature analysis: Classroom applications*. Newark, DE: International Reading Association.

Rupley, W.H., Logan, J.W., & Nichols, W.D. (1998–1999). Vocabulary instruction in a balanced reading program. *The Reading Teacher, 52*(4), 336–346.

Scott, J.A., Jamieson-Noel, D., & Asselin, M. (2003). Vocabulary instruction throughout the school day in 23 Canadian upper-elementary classrooms. *Elementary School Journal, 103*(3), 269–286.

Vygotsky, E. (1986). *Thought and language* (A. Kozalin, Trans.). Cambridge, MA: The MIT Press. (Original work published 1934)

LITERATURE CITED

Giblin, J. (2001). *Fireworks, picnics, and flags: The story of the Fourth of July symbols*. New York: Clarion Books.

Murphy, J. (2000). *Blizzard: The storm that changed America*. New York: Scholastic.

Schwartz, D.M. (2000). *Millions to measure*. Ill. S. Kellogg. New York: HarperCollins.

Sendak, M. (1963). *Where the wild things are*. New York: HarperTrophy.

CHAPTER 5

Fluency: An Oft-Neglected Goal of the Reading Program

Timothy V. Rasinski

MRS. HARRELSON, the school principal, and Ms. Barber, the school reading special-ist, meet to discuss summary data that Mrs. Harrelson recently received from Ms. Barber. Students in their elementary school had not performed well on the spring reading comprehension test mandated by the school district. Mrs. Harrelson had requested that Ms. Barber examine the nature of the difficulty that students were experiencing. Ms. Barber had arranged for classroom teachers in grades 2 through 5 to conduct one-minute reading surveys with their students.

Students had been asked to read a never-before-seen grade-level passage for one minute. Teachers then calculated the percentage of words students read accurately in the one-minute read and the total number of words read correctly in that minute. Along with this data, the teachers also noted the spring reading com-prehension test score for every student in their class.

Ms. Barber has compiled the results by grade level and submitted them to Mrs. Harrelson for her review. Mrs. Harrelson is puzzled by what she sees. For the most part, students were able to decode the words they encountered with a high degree of accuracy. At every grade level, students read, on average, with an accu-racy level of 94–96%—that is, students made about 4–6 errors for every 100 words read. This level of performance indicates a high degree of word decoding skill.

Understanding and Implementing Reading First Initiatives: The Changing Role of Administrators by Carrice Cummins, Editor. Copyright © 2006 by the International Reading Association.

Moreover, Mrs. Harrelson knows that the students are intelligent, have strong vocabularies, and appear to comprehend challenging texts read to them. She asks Ms. Barber if she might be able to shed some light on the situation.

What is the source of the students' reading difficulties? Ms. Barber, fresh from her master's program in reading, is indeed able to provide some insight into the data she has collected for Mrs. Harrelson: She explains that although the students are good decoders, they are not automatic decoders. This is reflected in students' reading rates (words read correct per minute) that were, on average, significantly below the norms that were expected of students at various grade levels (Rasinski, 2003, 2004). Ms. Barber explains that the students, although strong decoders with decent vocabularies and good comprehension skills, are not fluent readers. Many students had to analyze and consciously decode so many words and invested so much of their limited cognitive resources in word decoding that they did not have much left for making sense of the passage. Those students who were the slowest readers also tended to be the students most likely to perform poorly on the spring reading comprehension assessment.

Ms. Barber suggests that a portion of the time that is devoted to decoding and spelling instruction be given to reading fluency development, especially among those students who appear to demonstrate the greatest difficulties in this area. Mrs. Harrelson indicates that although she knows fluency is a "hot topic" in reading, she is not really sure what is meant by fluency or how it might be taught to students. She asks Ms. Barber to look at her calendar and find a mutually free hour in which she can bring her "up to speed" on reading fluency.

Defining Fluency

In its broadest sense, fluency refers to readers' mastery over the surface level of texts they read—the ability to accurately and effortlessly decode the written words and then to give meaning to those words through appropriate phrasing and oral expression of the words. When students are able to free their limited conscious cognitive resources from the mere task of decoding the words and concentrate more on meaning through oral interpretation and other active comprehension strategies, they are more likely to develop a satisfactory understanding of the texts they read.

Most adults not only are accurate decoders but also are fluent, or automatic, decoders. They are able to decode words so effortlessly that they can direct their interpretive skills to comprehending what they are reading. Very few words encountered by adult proficient readers require any conscious examination or analysis: A staggering majority of words are simply and instantly encountered and decoded without conscious attention. Moreover, when reading orally, adults use their cognitive resources to read aloud with appropriate and meaningful expression. This should be the goal for developing readers: to develop reading fluency so they can direct their conscious attention to the more important task of making sense of what they read.

Fluency is, in a sense, a bridge between phonics and word decoding on one hand, and vocabulary (word meaning) and comprehension (passage meaning) on the other. Fluency means making readers' decoding skills so automatic that they can focus on the meaning of the passage. Moreover, when readers read with fluency, they give evidence, through their oral interpretation of the text, that they are constructing meaning while they read. Recent examinations of research on reading fluency have concluded that fluency is essential to children's overall reading development (Chard, Vaughn, & Tyler, 2002; Kuhn & Stahl, 2000; National Institute of Child Health and Human Development, 2000; Rasinski & Hoffman, 2003). However, research also has indicated that a large portion of elementary students are not sufficiently fluent in their reading: One study indicated that nearly half of all fourth graders lack sufficient fluency to fully comprehend what they read (Pinnell et al., 1995). It has been this recent recognition of the importance of reading fluency that has led to its inclusion in the Reading First program and models of effective literacy instruction endorsed by Reading First, a part of the No Child Left Behind Act of 2001 (2002).

Reading instruction in the United States has undergone a dramatic shift as the federal government has mandated a course for literacy instruction in its Reading First program. Reading First mandates that literacy instruction be based on findings of scientific research, one of which has been that reading fluency is essential to students' overall reading growth and achievement. Thus, reading fluency instruction has been mandated for schools in the Reading First program.

Despite its inclusion in Reading First, reading fluency is perhaps the most misunderstood component of Reading First. As evidenced by the vignette, many educators are not familiar with fluency and how it might be incorporated in classroom instruction. Reading fluency has not, in the past, been an essential part of teacher training programs or programs for teaching reading (Rasinski & Zutell, 1996); yet, the research noted throughout this chapter clearly demonstrates its critical importance for instruction.

Once school administrators are aware of this important goal in reading instruction and learning, they are better able to support teachers who attempt to make reading fluency an integral part of their own classroom routines in reading. The remainder of this chapter outlines assessment and instructional strategies teachers can employ—and administrators can support—to attain the goal of fluent reading for all students.

Assessing Reading Fluency

There are a number of ways to assess reading fluency. Perhaps the easiest is to simply determine how fast a reader normally reads grade-appropriate text (Rasinski, 2004). Using this approach, often called an Oral Reading Fluency assessment, a teacher asks a student to read a never-before-seen grade-level passage for one minute. The teacher simply marks any uncorrected errors the student makes, as well as words that are provided to the student, and counts the number of words that are read correctly in the one-minute period. The student's performance is compared against grade-level reading rate norms (see Table 5.1). Students who perform significantly below the stated norms may be considered at risk in their reading fluency and overall reading development.

The Oral Reading Fluency assessment has the distinct advantage of being quick. It takes no more than a few minutes to assess a student's reading. The assessment has been shown to correlate remarkably well with other more general measures of reading achievement, including standardized tests (Rasinski, 2004). One note of caution, however, is worth mentioning. Although the Oral Reading Fluency assessment is a remarkably robust measure of the automaticity component of reading fluency, it is important that administrators, teachers, and students do

• Table 5.1 •
Oral Reading Fluency Assessment Target Rate Norms

Grade	wcpm* at Beginning of Year	wcpm at End of Year
1		30–60
2	30–60	70–100
3	50–90	80–110
4	70–110	100–140
5	80–120	110–150
6	100–140	120–160

* wcpm = words correct per minute

Rasinski, T.V. (2004). *Assessing reading fluency.* Honolulu, HI: Pacific Resources for Education and Learning. Retrieved September 3, 2005, from http://www.prel.org/products/re_/assessing-fluency.htm

not confuse this measure of fluency with good instruction. Although speed of reading is a good indicator of reading fluency, speed of reading should not normally be viewed as the aim of instructional efforts in reading. As a result of using this assessment, administrators, teachers, and students may conclude that direct instruction in increasing students' reading rate is the goal of fluency instruction. Direct instruction in reading rate may lead to faster reading, but it is questionable if it also will improve comprehension and overall reading performance. Most adults are quick, fluent readers who achieved their level of fluency without having to be subjected to speed-reading drills or invocations to read more quickly. Most adults who are fluent readers achieved fluency through practice. Specific kinds of practice for teaching fluency are presented in the next section of this chapter.

A MAP to Effective Fluency Instruction

Three key instructional strategies are essential to developing fluency in readers (Rasinski, 1989, 2003). The acronym MAP captures the essence of those strategies: (1) *model* fluent reading, (2) provide *assistance* while reading, and (3) provide opportunities for students to *practice* reading.

Model Fluency

Students need a solid idea of what is meant by reading fluency—that is, to read with appropriate accuracy, rate, and meaningful expression. This is perhaps best done by modeling for students what fluent reading looks like in the classroom, which means reading to students in meaningful and expressive ways. Administrators should make it a point to encourage daily oral reading to students by teachers. Students who are read to daily have larger vocabularies, better comprehension skills, a more positive attitude toward reading, and a more precise understanding of what it means to read with fluency (Rasinski, 2003). Not only should teachers read to students daily but also they should, from time to time, chat with their students about how expressively they themselves read and what makes for fluent and meaningful reading.

Assisted Reading

Assisted reading simply refers to the idea that children who are developing readers increase their reading fluency when they are provided prompt assistance by a more capable and more fluent reader who reads with them. The developing reader hears a fluent rendering of the passage while at the same time reading the text on his or her own. The simultaneous combination of seeing the words while hearing the words pronounced orally leads developing readers to improved and more expressive recognition of the words in text.

Assistance can take various forms. A teacher can read to a group of students while they follow along in their own books or on a story printed on the chalkboard or chart. A teacher or other more proficient reader (e.g., teacher aide, adult volunteer, older student, or principal) can sit beside a developing reader and together read aloud a text, the more advanced reader adjusting his or her voice to match the speed and proficiency of the developing reader. Ten to fifteen minutes of this sort of reading every day has been found to have a significant and positive effect on students' fluency, word recognition, and comprehension development (Topping, 1995).

Practice—Repeated Readings

Developing fluency in almost any endeavor, whether it is hitting a golf ball, playing a musical instrument, or driving a car, requires practice. This is true for reading as well. The more reading students do, the more automatic they become in recognizing words. As students become more effortless in decoding words, they are able to direct their attention to the more important task in reading—making sense of the passage, or comprehension.

One form of practice, repeated reading, has been found to be particularly important for developing reading fluency. Repeated reading refers to a reader reading a text several times, making multiple passes over it. Research has shown that as students engage in repeated readings they improve their ability to read the text practiced, but also, more important, they demonstrate improvement in reading passages they had never before seen, passages that may be more difficult than the ones practiced. This transfer of learning from one text to another suggests that engaging students in this sort of repeated practice is one of the best ways to develop reading fluency and overall reading proficiency.

Repeated reading can manifest itself in a variety of ways in classrooms. Perhaps the most authentic use of repeated readings occurs when students are asked to practice reading texts that will eventually be performed for others. If students know they will be performing their assigned passages, they will have a natural reason for practicing them.

Many texts lend themselves to performance and practice. These include scripts performed as Readers Theatre (Martinez, Roser, & Strecker,

1998–1999), monologues and dialogues, poetry and rhymes, song lyrics, speeches and notable quotations, well wishes, jokes and riddles, and cheers. The employment of repeated readings with these types of texts usually begins with the students choosing or the teacher assigning an appropriate text early in the week. Students then spend short periods of time throughout the week practicing the text—by themselves, with their classmates, under the guidance of the teacher or parent, in school, or at home. At or near the end of the week, the teacher provides a time for students to perform their assigned passage for an audience of classmates. Parents and other guests are often invited to performances such as poetry slams, Readers Theatre festivals, or other weekly performances that allow students to demonstrate their abilities to convey meaning and feeling in their reading and gain a well-deserved sense of accomplishment.

Teacher coaching is a critical part of repeated readings activities. As students practice a passage, they need formative feedback that will help them shape their reading to the appropriate and desired level of meaningful expression. Teachers should be the primary source of this coaching in the classroom as they listen to their students read, model appropriate reading of the passage, and provide encouragement and feedback to student readers. Most students only need minutes per day to gain the insight and self-confidence from teachers that will move them toward fluent reading. Later, as students themselves and others become familiar with the type of coaching that leads to expressive reading, they can provide this critical assistance to other students.

Many of the texts recommended for repeated readings represent genres of literature that have recently become neglected in the elementary school reading curriculum. Poetry and song, for example, have been traditional mainstays of the elementary reading curriculum; yet in recent years they have fallen out of favor as reading curriculum developers focus their efforts on texts that are more likely to have an impact on students' test performance. However, these types of texts are a legitimate part of the elementary literature canon and should be included in a comprehensive literacy curriculum for the elementary grades. By bringing these types of texts back into the reading curriculum, teachers will provide a richer literacy experience for their students and simultaneously lay the groundwork for authentic and engaging repeated readings.

Synergistic Fluency Instruction

Modeling, providing assistance, and practice in reading are three building blocks for effective reading fluency instruction. Individually implemented, they will help students become aware of the concept of reading fluency and work to make themselves more fluent readers. When teachers can combine these building blocks into a seamless instructional routine, they will create a fluency synergy in which the effects of the routine itself will be greater than the sum of the parts of the instruction. One such fluency routine is the Fluency Development Lesson (FDL).

Rasinski, Padak, Linek, and Sturtevant (1994) and Rasinski and Padak (2004) developed the FDL in response to a need for more direct and systematic instruction in reading fluency. Each brief daily lesson includes fluency modeling, assisted reading, repeated readings, and word study with a text that is meant to be performed. In addition, the lesson is intended for use at home as well as in school. The lesson can be particularly effective with students who have not achieved sufficient levels of fluency at any grade level. The format for the FDL is as follows:

1. The teacher provides each student with two copies of a poem or other text for that day's lesson.

2. The teacher reads aloud the passage two to three times to students in an expressive and meaningful way. Students follow along silently.

3. The teacher and students discuss the passage as well as the teacher's reading of the passage.

4. Teacher and students chorally read the passage two or three times.

5. Students are paired off and practice the passage three times each with their partners. One student reads the passage three times while the partner follows along silently, provides help when needed, and offers encouragement and praise for his or her partner's reading. Then, students switch roles.

6. Individually, in pairs, or in small groups, students perform the assigned passage for their classmates or other audiences determined by the teacher.

7. Students and teachers select three to five words from the passage to add to a class word chart. These words are discussed and used in later word study activities, including word analysis and practice, word games, and word sorts.

8. Students put one copy of their poem in their class poetry folders for later practice and performance. Another copy is sent home. Students are encouraged to read the passage repeatedly to their parents, siblings, and other family members. Some teachers have

created a Lucky Listener program in which persons who listen to the students read can sign the reverse side of the paper on which the passage is printed. Students can compete to bring in to class the most "autographs" from the previous night's home reading.

9. On the next day, a new lesson begins with a new passage. However, before beginning the new passage, teachers often ask students to read the previous day's passage.

The FDL provides authentic opportunities for students to listen to fluent reading and to practice reading with assistance and to an audience—thus incorporating the critical features of the MAP fluency model. Research has shown that it can positively affect students' reading performance (Rasinski et al., 1994).

The Administrator's Role in Fluency Instruction

Principals and other school and district administrators can promote fluency instruction in a number of ways. First, they need to make reading fluency a priority in their schools. Too often, it has been the case that fluency has not been adequately taught in elementary schools. As previously mentioned, recent research has demonstrated that fluency is indeed critical to fluency success and that it must be an integral part of the reading curriculum at every grade level.

Fluency should be a critical topic for the school's professional learning community. Administrators must also ensure that teachers have adequate and ongoing education and training in the MAP fluency instruction model, the FDL, and other aspects of effective fluency instruction, including fluency assessment. Effective fluency instruction does not happen overnight, nor does it happen with a single professional development session. Once it becomes a priority for the school, administrators must provide systematic and ongoing education and training in reading fluency, which should include direct training from others knowledgeable on the topic, professional reading and peer discussions on fluency, analyses of results from fluency assessments, planning for fluency instruction, developing and acquiring materials for fluency instruction, coaching of teachers engaged in fluency instruction, and opportunities for teachers to interact with other teachers around fluency and observe other more experienced teachers in their implementation of fluency instruction.

Principals and other administrators also should work to ensure that parents are made aware of the importance of fluency and the MAP fluency model, encouraged to use it with their children regularly, and are supported in using it with their children. Administrators also can lead efforts to develop parental volunteer efforts in the school aimed at fluency. Fluency practice often requires nothing more than an encouraging and supportive adult to listen to children read for 15–20 minutes at a time. A school volunteer fluency program in which parents read to, read with, and listen to children read is a natural way for parents who do not have specialized training to provide effective reading support for children in the school.

Effective reading instruction is a data-driven process. Administrators need to develop procedures for obtaining, analyzing, reporting, and using reading fluency data from students over the years. This data can show trends in fluency achievement as well as concerns at certain grade levels or in particular classrooms and lead to effective interventions that will improve the overall reading achievement of students.

Curriculum-based reading assessment is one way to obtain this data (Rasinski, 2004; Rasinski & Padak, 2005a, 2005b). At three or four regularly scheduled points throughout the school year (e.g., September, December, March, and May), students are individually assessed by their teacher or other literacy professional. Students are asked to read orally a short grade-level passage, followed by an unprompted retelling of the passage. From this brief activity (usually 3–4 minutes) teachers can check students' decoding accuracy (percentage of words read correctly), oral reading fluency (total number of words read correctly in the first minute of reading), and comprehension (retelling that is scored against a descriptive rubric). This data allows teachers to track student progress on three key indicators of reading success across the school year and, most important, identify those students who do not appear to be making adequate progress and who might benefit from more intensive or supplemental intervention instruction.

Finally, administrators can employ the MAP methodology in their own work with children. Principals are the instructional leaders of their schools. The very best principals continue to be teachers at heart in their buildings. The modeling, assistance, and practicing nature of effective fluency instruction provides principals and other administrators with wonderful opportunities to work with students directly—reading to them regularly in a fluent and expressive manner, sitting side by side with selected students in an assisted-reading format, and being an enthusiastic audience for students performing texts they have practiced. These all are simple but powerful ways that administrators can nurture fluency for students and model effective fluency instruction for faculty, parents, and others.

Conclusion

Although reading fluency has been on the backburner of reading programs for many years, it is finally being recognized as essential to students' reading success. Although it is up to teachers to make fluency instruction happen in their classrooms, it is critical that school administrators understand the concept of reading fluency and how it can be nurtured in school and at home. Principals, as their schools' instructional leaders, help set the instructional priorities in their buildings and they explain and justify those priorities to parents, the central administration, and the general public. Principals and school administrators, then, are a key for making fluency instruction authentic, engaging, and effective for all students. If we make this oft-neglected goal of reading an integral part of the school reading curriculum, I am certain we will realize the potential for helping huge numbers of students achieve their full potential in reading and across the school curriculum.

REFERENCES

Chard, D.J., Vaughn, S., & Tyler, B. (2002). A synthesis of research on effective interventions for building reading fluency with elementary students with learning disabilities. *Journal of Learning Disabilities, 35*(5), 386–406.

Kuhn, M.R., & Stahl, S.A. (2000). *Fluency: A review of developmental and remedial practices* (CIERA Rep. No. 2-008). Ann Arbor, MI: Center for the Improvement of Early Reading Achievement.

Martinez, M., Roser, N., & Strecker, S. (1998–1999). "I never thought I could be a star": A reader's theatre ticket to reading fluency. *The Reading Teacher, 52*(4), 326–334.

National Institute of Child Health and Human Development. (2000). *Report of the National Reading Panel. Teaching children to read: An evidence-based assessment of the scientific research literature on reading and its implications for reading instruction* (NIH Publication No. 00-4769). Washington, DC: U.S. Government Printing Office.

No Child Left Behind Act of 2001, Pub. L No. 107-110, 115 Stat. 1425 (2002). Retrieved October 1, 2005, from http://edworkforce.house.gov/issues/107th/education/nclb/nclb.htm

Pinnell, G.S., Pikulski, J.J., Wixson, K.K., Campbell, J.R., Gough, P.B., & Beatty, A.S. (1995). *Listening to children read aloud.* Washington, DC: U.S. Department of Education, Office of Educational Research and Improvement.

Rasinski, T.V. (1989). Fluency for everyone: Incorporating fluency instruction in the classroom. *The Reading Teacher, 42*(9), 690–693.

Rasinski, T.V. (2003). *The fluent reader: Oral reading strategies for building word recognition, fluency, and comprehension.* New York: Scholastic.

Rasinski, T.V. (2004). *Assessing reading fluency.* Honolulu, HI: Pacific Resources for Education and Learning. Retrieved September 3, 2005, from http://www.prel.org/products/re_/assessing-fluency.htm

Rasinski, T.V., & Hoffman, T.V. (2003). Theory and research into practice: Oral reading in the school literacy curriculum. *Reading Research Quarterly, 38*(4), 510–522.

Rasinski, T.V., & Padak, N. (2004). *Fluency first! Grade levels K–3: Daily routines to develop reading fluency.* Chicago: The Wright Group.

Rasinski, T.V., & Padak, N. (2005a). *Three-minute reading assessments (grades 1–4): Word recognition, fluency, and comprehension.* New York: Scholastic.

Rasinski, T.V., & Padak, N. (2005b). *Three-minute reading assessments (grades 5–8): Word recognition, fluency, and comprehension.* New York: Scholastic.

Rasinski, T.V., Padak, N.D., Linek, W.L., & Sturtevant, E. (1994). Effects of fluency development on urban second-grade readers. *Journal of Educational Research, 87*(3), 158–165.

Rasinski, T.V., & Zutell, J.B. (1996). Is fluency yet a goal of the reading curriculum? In E.G. Sturtevant & W.M. Linek (Eds.), *Growing literacy* (18th yearbook of the College Reading Association, pp. 237–246). Harrisonburg, VA: College Reading Association.

Topping, K. (1995). *Paired reading, spelling, and writing: The handbook for teachers and parents.* New York: Cassell.

CHAPTER 6

Comprehension Instruction: Research-Based Practices

Cathy Collins Block

AT THE BEGINNING of the school year, Mr. Hamilton, a first-year elementary school principal, tells his staff that he will visit all teachers in the school as they teach reading. He wants to observe newly developed research-based comprehension practices in action. He also wants to ensure that each grade level's lesson advances the learning that occurred in the students' previous years of instruction. Mr. Hamilton states that while he is visiting, he will talk to individual students regarding what they do to comprehend text. As Mr. Hamilton observes Mr. Sullivan, he talks to Roberto, a bright second grader whose parents do not speak English. Roberto tells him,

> I never liked reading when I was in first grade. I couldn't understand things. Then, Mr. Sullivan taught me how to think for myself and follow what an author was saying. Because of Mr. Sullivan, I can come to the end of a story and already be thinking about the ending before the author tells it to me. Mr. Sullivan says I can do this because I am using good comprehension processes. Now that I'm with Mr. Sullivan, I love to read. Reading is my favorite class, and I can remember what I'm reading. I no longer just call out words and act like I know what the words are saying when I really don't understand.

Understanding and Implementing Reading First Initiatives: The Changing Role of Administrators by Carrice Cummins, Editor. Copyright © 2006 by the International Reading Association.

When the 2005–2006 school year began, 54% of the students enrolled in Texas public schools came from homes in which the primary language was not English or homes in which the caregivers were from non-Caucasian ethnic backgrounds. This event marked the first time in U.S. history that Texas educators, like their counterparts in many other regions of the country, experienced the phenomenon that the traditionally minority public school population became the majority population in their schools. As a result, teaching students to comprehend English as a second language is becoming a more frequent challenge faced by more administrators as they work to build the literacy skills of all students in their buildings.

The research-based lessons described in this chapter can provide instruction upon which administrators can depend to significantly increase the comprehension abilities of the diverse student populations that are present in schools today (Block, Rodgers, & Johnson, 2004). Reading First, a part of the No Child Left Behind Act of 2001 (2002), also has provided resources to assist all children to learn how to comprehend. This chapter is designed to provide administrators with increased information concerning highly effective, best practices for comprehension development. Specifically, the objectives of this chapter are to

- assist administrators and teachers in understanding and using the newest research-based comprehension instructional practices;

- provide sample lessons for administrators to share with teachers who want new methods to build the comprehension abilities of English-language learners, as well as students who are reading above grade level, on grade level, and below their grade-level placements;

- provide an outline of scientifically validated comprehension methods that administrators, principals, assistant principals, literacy coaches, lead teachers, and literacy coordinators can recommend to teachers after having observed reading instruction in individual classrooms; and

- enable primary-grade teachers to build a strong, lifelong foundation for all children's literacy success.

Defining and Explaining Research–Based Comprehension Practices

Reading comprehension is defined by Reading First legislation as "the act or result of applying comprehension processes to obtain the meaning from a graphic or textual communication" (National Institute of Child Health and

Human Development [NICHD], 2000, p. 4–3). To understand text, readers must (a) comprehend the literal meaning printed on the page, (b) interpret authors' implied meanings, and (c) evaluate and apply ideas in printed materials to their lives (Harris & Hodges, 1995). The National Reading Panel Report of 2000 (NRP; NICHD) followed these definitions as they conducted a critical review of comprehension research. The resultant analysis identified 38 studies of specific instructional approaches that demonstrated to significantly increase young children's comprehension.

Prior to the NRP's review of research and Reading First legislation, some educators thought that comprehension instruction should be delayed until after students had mastered basic decoding skills. Today, we know that the opposite is true. By teaching comprehension strategies early in children's lives, we can advance not only their abilities to understand text but also their decoding skills and reading fluency skills (Block & Israel, 2004).

Recent research also has found that the ability to understand text is a complex process that develops over time (Block, 1999; Chall, 1998; Collins, 1991; Pearson & Fielding, 1991), and comprehension abilities differ from other major reading competencies described in previous chapters in this volume (i.e., phonemic awareness and phonics). Decoding skills can be mastered through highly effective teachers' instruction, and once their basic learning principles are known, most students can automatically use their basic skills to decode novel words. However, the ability to comprehend increasingly complex text can never occur by merely mastering a basic set of skills. Because every sentence is a unique and new creation, comprehension requires that students continuously develop more and more advanced comprehension competencies and that students continuously apply their focused attention and self-guided thinking throughout every reading experience.

To develop these abilities, students must have instruction in (a) comprehension strategies and processes as well as how to select the ones that they will need to understand increasingly complex texts; (b) how to use textual features (e.g., subheadings, textbook organizational features, indexes, table of contents, and so forth) to follow an author's train of thought; and (c) how to think about their own thinking while they read. This instruction must also help them learn how to *want* to correct confusions, tie new information to prior knowledge, and apply relevant information to their lives. Because of all these complexities, primary educators should continuously and systematically add depth and breadth to the number of comprehension processes students learn. For example, a lesson that teaches students to use authorial clues to draw conclusions while they read should not look the same in first and third grades. As texts become more complex, teachers' modeling, direct instruction, and the number of processes that teachers ask students to independently apply in their reading should increase substantially. That is, the same explanation and lesson for how to use a Venn diagram should not be seen in kindergarten, first, second, and third grade.

One of the most important actions primary-grade teachers can take to build students' comprehension skills is teaching three different types, or strands, of comprehension lessons each year. These lessons develop literal, inferential, and metacognitive comprehension skills.

Literal comprehension is the ability to understand the exact meaning of words and sentences that the author wrote. Students also must recognize the way in which the author orders information throughout the text. Primary-grade students should learn several literal comprehension processes such as identifying main ideas, recognizing cause-and-effect relations, connecting details, following a sequence, and using the format and layout of a text to gain meaning.

Inferential comprehension requires students to gain meaning from text when that meaning is not directly stated. Inferential comprehension abilities enable students to recognize and move beyond an author's purpose and to combine literal comprehension with their own thoughts (Cain-Thoreson, Lippman, & McClendon-Magnuson, 1997; Pressley & Afflerbach, 1995). This form of comprehension is not a one-step process. It requires students to create mental pictures, think intently about a text, relate it to their personal experiences, and connect it to other information that they just read or that they have learned previously (Baker, 2002; Block & Johnson, 2002; Kintsch, 1999; Omanson, Warren, & Trabasso, 1978). Inferential skills that primary-grade students should learn are how to infer, draw conclusions, follow an author's train of thought, predict, connect main events to characters' motives, and interpret.

Metacognitive comprehension involves thinking about one's own thinking before, during, and after reading. It also includes the "skill and will" (Paris, Wasik, & Turner, 1991) to overcome one's own reading challenges. Metacognitive processes help students to (a) remove decoding, fluency, and vocabulary difficulties that interrupt comprehension; (b) reflect on what they have learned and what they want to learn next; and (c) apply relevant, valid information to their lives independently. Most students must receive explicit metacognitive process instruction or they will not learn how to engage these processes independently (Baker, 2002; Block, 1998, 2000; Block & Pressley, 2002; Keene & Zimmermann, 1997; Paris et al., 1991). When primary-grade readers become more metacognitive comprehenders, they make more connections between their understanding; the textual content; and their own knowledge, expectations, and purposes for reading (Block & Whiteley, in press).

Research has firmly established that many students cannot develop these three types of comprehension processes unaided (Block, Gambrell, & Pressley, 2004; Block, Rodgers, et al., 2004; Chall, 1998; Durkin, 1978–1979). In addition, children who cannot comprehend "tend to fall further behind their peers [in their comprehension abilities] by third grade, regardless of their mastery of decoding skills" (Chall, 1998, p. 98). The NRP also found that to be the most effective, comprehension instruction must contain (a) direct instruction, (b) expanded teacher explanations, and (c) transactional strategy instruction—that is, teacher's explanations of comprehension processes, with graphics to depict them, and highly effective monitoring of an individual student's applications of comprehension processes to text.

To ensure that all primary-grade students receive the best comprehension instruction, students should experience three different types of comprehension lessons each year. When they do, their performances on measures of literal, inferential, and metacognitive comprehension increase as each type or strand of lesson systematically increases the number, depth, and breadth of comprehension processes students learn how to independently apply while they read. These three types of comprehension lessons also have proven to increase students' vocabulary, decoding, problem solving, cooperative group skills, and self-esteem as determined by the Iowa Test of Basic Skills, the Harter Test of Self-Concept, informal reading inventories, and standardized reasoning tests (Block, 1999; Block & Whiteley, in press; Collins, 1991).

Further, when these three distinct types of comprehension lessons are included, the instructional program is referred to as Comprehension Process Instruction (CPI). CPI lessons combine direct, expanded teacher direction with transactional strategy instruction through the use of print-rich, developmentally appropriate textual experiences that actively engage students' independent thinking. In so doing, even the youngest readers can learn how to untangle confusions and overcome the complexities in print and technology that could have blocked their understanding.

Comprehension Process Instruction

Prior to 1990, many teachers taught comprehension by (1) giving directions, (2) telling students to "read carefully," (3) assigning workbook pages, or (4) asking literal questions after a text was read. In 1991, Pearson and Fielding argued for a movement away from these time-honored traditions. They described how teachers should teach comprehension—not as a set of skills but rather as a series of strategic processes. At that time, only a few educators were highly skilled in demonstrating and explaining comprehension as thought processes (what Paris et al., 1991, labeled "making thinking public," p. 173). Today, through scientifically validated CPI, many teachers have developed the abilities to explain and teach a wide variety of comprehension processes (Block, 2003; Block & Mangieri, 1995–1996, 2003; Block, Rodgers, et al., 2004). CPI also is enabling great numbers of less able readers to practice their comprehension abilities in real-world situations, even if their current reading levels are below their grade-level placements.

The three types of comprehension lessons are (1) teacher-directed lessons that include rich, engaging demonstrations of comprehension processes in action (Strand 1 lessons); (2) lessons conducted in one-on-one settings in which the student reads silently and applies what he or she has learned in a Strand 1 lesson while the teacher provides individualized, direct instruction at specific points in a text where personal comprehension difficulties arise (Strand 2 lessons); and (3) lessons in which students choose which comprehension process they want and need to learn more about (Strand 3 lessons). Strand 3 lessons produce highly significant gains in children's understanding because young readers become more metacognitively aware and motivated to learn because they are involved in choosing what is important for them to learn next to improve their reading abilities (Block, Rodgers, et al., 2004).

Strand 1, 2, and 3 lessons occur in a cycle, with Strand 1 lessons beginning the cycle. Teachers teach Strand 1 lessons for as many days as needed until students can use a process independently. Then, the CPI program moves to a Strand 2 lesson. In Strand 2 lessons, teachers ask students to practice initiating the comprehension process(es) just taught while they read silently or independently. At this stage of the cycle, students engage in independent reading experiences, and their teachers provide one-on-one instruction at an exact point in a text where a student experiences confusion. Teachers continue Strand 2 lessons until students can determine (a) which steps in the comprehension process they do well, (b) which aspects of their comprehension could be improved, and (c) what types of texts make it easy or difficult for them to independently initiate the specific comprehension process(es) taught in the Strand 1 lessons. For example, when a student can use the information the teacher provided in a Strand 2 lesson about how to identify authors' main ideas (literal comprehension) to predict the conclusion of one fictional story before the author states it (inferential comprehension) but realizes that it is difficult to do so in other fiction and nonfiction books, he or she is ready to move on to a Strand 3 lesson.

At this point in the CPI cycle, students are taught how to assess their own specific comprehension strengths and weaknesses. Afterward, their newly discovered comprehension needs become the basis for planning the next Strand 1 lesson, and the CPI instructional cycle begins anew.

Strand 1 Lessons: Providing Direct Teacher Instruction

The goal of each Strand 1 lesson is to preteach students how to make meaning. Strand 1 lessons follow the effective comprehension strategy instructional model identified by the NRP (NICHD, 2000). In these lessons, teachers describe, in depth, how to use a specific comprehension process such as drawing conclusions, making inferences, identifying cause and effect relations, and finding the main idea. Strand 1 lessons begin by teachers providing direct explanations of one or more comprehension processes (depending on students' grade levels and ability levels). Teachers follow these explanations with three demonstrations of how to use each of the processes at three different points in a text in which the specific processes could help students understand that text. Then, teachers model how they performed each comprehension process by telling students what they thought while reading at these three points in the text. This process of "telling one's thoughts" is called a think-aloud.

Traditionally, a think-aloud is performed when teachers read aloud sentences and then stop the reading to describe what they were thinking (as they read that text) and how they applied one or more of the comprehension processes at that point in the text to gain meaning. (See Block & Israel, 2004, for examples of think-alouds for 15 comprehension processes.) To illustrate this point, if a teacher is teaching first-grade students how to identify a main idea, the teacher would describe what a main idea is, why main ideas are important, and how main ideas differ from other detail-specific sentences. Then, the teacher would show on an overhead projector three paragraphs from a text that students are about to read. Next, the teacher would demonstrate how he or she found the main idea sentence by reading each paragraph separately and performing a think-aloud about what he or she thought to find each main idea sentence.

The next step in a Strand 1 lesson is for teachers to scaffold (or support) the class as all students try to use the comprehension process just taught. Usually, teachers ask the entire class to read a new set of sentences. Then, the class stops reading at a point in the sentences when students should use the comprehension process just taught. The teacher then asks a few students to describe what they were thinking at that point in the text to comprehend, and how they used the process just taught to increase their comprehension. For example, a teacher could demonstrate how to draw a conclusion from a set of sentences. Then, he or she could ask everyone in the class to read the next section from a poem, textbook, or trade book. When students have read enough to draw a second conclusion, the teacher could stop the class and ask a few students to describe how they drew a conclusion, using the information that the class had just read. In this manner, Strand 1 lessons enable teachers to provide expanded explanations of new comprehension processes. They also enable students to hear several teacher and peer think-alouds to guide them as they try to use the processes for the first time.

The content of Strand 1 lessons include teacher demonstrations of how to

- set a purpose for reading;
- find main ideas, causes and effects, and relevant details;
- infer, predict, make connections, gain different perspectives, and reason as they read;
- reflect, sum up, visualize, draw conclusions, and ask questions before, during, and after reading;
- use prior knowledge gained in life and (through the reading of prior sentences in a text) to comprehend upcoming statements;
- fill the gaps in an author's writing by "tilling a text" (Block, 2003), which is to use titles, subtitles, boldface text, and other graphic features in a book to gain meaning;
- monitor one's own reading to identify when comprehension has and has not occurred; and
- reread, gain perspectives different from one's life, and apply the meaning in the text to one's life.

Teachers should conclude Strand 1 lessons by reminding students to think about what their minds are doing to help them comprehend and use that process independently. These five questions have one characteristic in common. They cannot be answered unless students comprehended the text. Questions such as, "What did you like about this book?" can be answered whether or not the student understood the text. Such questions as this do not improve all students' abilities to use comprehension processes (Block, 2003). The teacher also asks literal, interpretive, application, and metacognitive comprehension questions. These questions can be similar to the following:

- How did the comprehension process we just learned help you as you read?
- How did it help you think ahead, clarify, and remember?
- How did it help you stay involved in the story?
- How did it help you overcome distractions in the room?
- How did it help you overcome confusion in the text?

In summary, every Strand 1 lesson provides teacher-directed instruction of a comprehension process. Strand 1 lessons begin by teachers identifying a literary process that students need to comprehend a particular text. The teacher then selects a text and prepares three demonstrations of the thinking processes using a graphic or kinesthetic guide and/or think-alouds. Next, the teacher and students read orally or silently from a text. After reading, teachers ask students to describe how, where, and why they used the comprehension process being taught.

For example, one type of Strand 1 lesson uses Comprehension Process Motions (CPM). This lesson involves using a kinesthetic thinking guide in the form of hand motions. These hand motions, CPMs, provide kinesthetic and tactical depictions of the silent, unobservable mental processes that must be engaged for a student to comprehend text. These motions can be displayed on posters and referenced during the first three teacher demonstrations as well as the whole-class practice sessions in Strand 1 lessons. Twelve CPMs have been shown to significantly increase students' understanding of important comprehension abilities (Block, in press). Figure 6.1 shows one of the CPMs; one that can be used to teach students how to draw conclusions. (See Block, Rodgers, et al., 2004, for additional CPM charts.)

A second type of Strand 1 lesson uses a graphic thinking guide in the form of a table. Thinking guides are available from commercial publishers, such as the ones that appear in Block and Mangieri (1995–1996), or they can be teacher-constructed graphic aids. Each thinking guide displays the steps and processes that teachers want students to use when they initiate a comprehension process, such as setting a purpose, making an inference, drawing a conclusion, identifying the causes and effects, and recognize relevant details. It would show the three steps in the inference process.

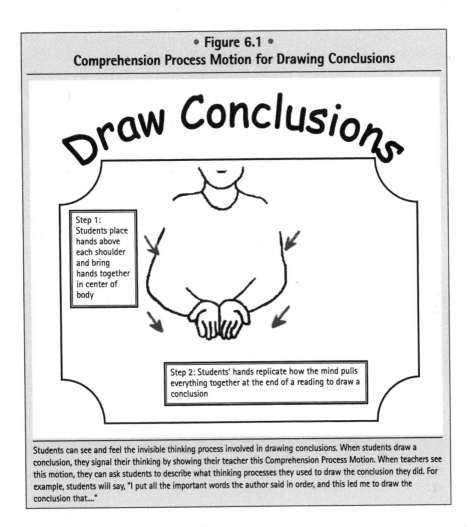

• Figure 6.1 •
Comprehension Process Motion for Drawing Conclusions

Draw Conclusions

Step 1: Students place hands above each shoulder and bring hands together in center of body

Step 2: Students' hands replicate how the mind pulls everything together at the end of a reading to draw a conclusion

Students can see and feel the invisible thinking process involved in drawing conclusions. When students draw a conclusion, they signal their thinking by showing their teacher this Comprehension Process Motion. When teachers see this motion, they can ask students to describe what thinking processes they used to draw the conclusion they did. For example, students will say, "I put all the important words the author said in order, and this led me to draw the conclusion that...."

Each step would become the heading for each of the three columns of the table. These columns would read as follows: (1) Think About What I Read + (2) Think About What I Learned and Thought About While I Read = (3) Infer What the Author Means. Teachers describe each step they thought as they read. Then, they write their thoughts in all three columns on the teaching guide. This is an example for students and is completed three times before teachers ask students to explain their thoughts for each step in the inference process, using subsequent paragraphs in the same texts used by the teacher.

A third method of teaching Strand 1 lessons involves the think-aloud described earlier in this chapter. Teachers model and repeatedly perform think-alouds, and then ask students to report through the think-alouds the comprehension process they used at a particular point in a text to understand the author's meaning. For example, in the identifying the main idea activity described earlier in this chapter, a teacher read all the sentences in a paragraph and then performed the think-aloud: "I knew that the sentence 'All trees have roots' was the main idea because main idea sentences have all-encompassing words like *all* in them and because all the other sentences in this paragraph give a detail that tells about roots, which is the most important topic of this paragraph."

In summary, Strand 1 lessons include teachers telling students how they and other expert readers make meaning while they read. Strand 1 lessons provide the direct instruction that helps students understand how to use the "teachers within" (i.e., metacognitive thinking, prior experiences, and personal goals) and the "teachers without" (i.e., teachers, peers, and textual clues as well as printed, visual, and oral media context and format clues) to comprehend (Cain-Thoreson et al., 1997; Pressley & Afflerbach, 1995).

Sample Strand 1 Lesson: Setting a Purpose and Inferring

In the following Strand 1 lesson, teachers help students to think about two comprehension processes while they read.

Objective of the Lesson

Students set their own purposes prior to reading and infer while they read.

Materials

Text or story that can be read by all students

Procedure

1. The teacher describes (a) how students can set their own purposes prior to reading and make inferences while they read, and (b) how the processes will help them become better readers.

2. The teacher reads two pages of a text and does a think-aloud that shows students how they set their purpose for reading. Then, the teacher asks students to state their purposes.

3. The teacher puts a sticky note on the bottom of page 3 of a new book that he or she gives to each student. The teacher asks each student to read from page 1 to page 3 and then write his or her purpose for reading on in the book on the sticky note.

4. Students share what they wrote on the sticky notes with the class so students can learn how different people set different purposes for reading the same book.

5. For younger readers, the teacher and students read to the end of the book and the teacher completes these five steps repeatedly until students understand that they are to set a purpose for reading at the beginning of each book. For older students, the teacher reminds students of the inference process that had been taught on a previous day. The teacher describes the steps in the inference process and demonstrates how to infer using the three-column thinking guide described earlier in this chapter.

6. The teacher again explains and reminds students that he or she was able to infer things by using clues from the way the author wrote the first three pages by how fast the author introduced new topics and by the choice of words that the author used. Then, the teacher asks students to (a) place a second sticky note on the bottom of page 4, (b) read the page, and (c) then write their inferences regarding what they think will occur on page 5 on the sticky note.

7. Students share the inferences that they wrote on their thinking notes and describe why they thought their inferences were correct. Then, everyone in the class reads page 5.

8. After reading page 5, the teacher asks a few students to state why their inferences were correct or incorrect.

9. This process continues as students read subsequent pages. If a student's inference was correct, that student places a checkmark on the back of the sticky note along with his or her name or initials. If a student's inference was wrong, that student puts an X on the back of the sticky note along with his or her name or initials and what the student did not do in the inference process. Students turn in completed sticky notes to the teacher.

10. On the next day, students who wrote checkmarks work as a group with a more difficult text, and they continue to read (this time silently) and write their inferences on paper or more sticky notes for the next pages before they read them. Those students who wrote Xs work with the teacher in a small group to relearn the inference comprehension process. The teacher follows the above steps again with these students.

Strand 2 Lessons: Delivering Mini-Interventions at Points of Need

The goal of Strand 2 lessons is to provide more time for students to (a) practice engaging the comprehension processes learned in Strand 1 while they read independently, (b) ask for one-on-one mini-interventions from their teachers when they cannot initiate these processes independently, and (c) enjoy reading more books at school. Strand 2 lessons teach students to stop and ask for help when confusions arise. These lessons differ from traditional silent reading periods because students are told to raise their hands when they come to a point in a text when they do not understand something. At these times, the teacher conducts a mini-intervention with each student to demonstrate how he or she knew which process to use to make meaning. A mini-intervention occurs quickly (lasting about 30 seconds to one minute) so students can return to the enjoyment of engaging in a meaningful, silent reading experience. Many teachers elect peer volunteers to assist them during Strand 2 lessons so students can receive mini-interventions more rapidly and more student needs can be met.

Using Strand 2 lessons also enables students to move to higher levels of understanding more frequently because their teachers and peer leaders become personal coaches who are at their sides whenever the students become frustrated or confused.

Sample Strand 2 Lesson: Helping Students Overcome Individual Comprehension Problems

The following sample of a Strand 2 lesson is designed to provide time during a silent reading period for students to practice the inference process taught in the Strand 1 lesson described earlier in this chapter.

Objective of the Lesson
Students learn how and when to infer while they read silently or independently.

Materials
Books selected by the teacher or students

Procedure

1. The teacher asks students to select a book and read silently.

2. The teacher assists students who raise their hands when they encounter confusion by providing a one-on-one instructional intervention. In this mini-intervention, the teacher says one sentence to provide the meaning of a sentence that has confused the student and follows this statement with a second sentence to briefly reteach the inference comprehension process.

3. Immediately after leaving this student's desk, the teacher records that the inference process was retaught to this student. This anecdotal record also documents the specific type of text that caused this individual to experience difficulty with inferential comprehension.

Strand 3 Lessons: Assessing Comprehension Strengths and Weaknesses

The goal of Strand 3 lessons is to teach students how to identify their comprehension strengths and weaknesses. These lessons are important because students themselves are most aware of the level of effort and the amount of drive that they are willing to expend to become better readers. The outcome of Strand 3 lessons is to increase this level of effort and drive, metacognition, and the desire to *want* to overcome reading obstacles.

Strand 3 lessons elicit and foster students' metacognitive, intentional, and deliberate thoughts about their own comprehension abilities. It also (a) increases their abilities to select and combine appropriate comprehension processes when the need arises during independent reading opportunities, (b) elicits students' ideas about how they could become better readers, (c) enables students to make new discoveries about themselves as readers, and (d) enhances their abilities to seek out and read more difficult text as they overcome larger comprehension challenges (Block, 2003; Block & Whiteley, in press). Strand 3 lessons also can allow students to choose what they want to learn about the reading process, not simply what they want to learn next about a particular topic.

Recent studies have demonstrated that although good and poor comprehenders use similar comprehension processes, good comprehenders are willing to persist in using and adapting the same and more advanced processes until they determine the meaning in a text (Afflerbach, 2002). Without Strand 3 lessons, poorer readers tend to (a) reuse very few comprehension processes, (b) attempt to comprehend every text using the same limited set of comprehension processes, and (c) read less often because comprehending becomes a frustrating task that they avoid (Block & Pressley, 2002). Moreover, when Strand 3 lessons are not included in elementary reading programs, students' abilities to discover and savor subtle meanings in text remain untapped, which in turn limits their capacity to kindle deeper emotional responses.

Strand 3 lessons also provide opportunities for students to discuss new methods they are using to make meaning and to identify what they want to learn next to comprehend better. In these lessons, students tell their teachers and peers which skills and strategies they use to read text, as well as what kind of help they need to comprehend material more completely and efficiently. Strand 3 lessons also enable students to ask more questions of themselves, such as the following:

- What processes do I need to comprehend more difficult fiction and nonfiction?
- What did I learn to do this week to comprehend better?
- What is bothering me about my reading abilities?
- What thinking processes did I elicit at a particular point in this text to create a more complete understanding, and how did they help me?

Sample Strand 3 Lesson: Students Assessing How Well They Inferred

Strand 3 lessons are conducted as whole-class or small-group conversations. When the entire class is involved, students and their teacher sit in a circle facing one another. In this lesson, students choose to discuss the inference comprehension process that they learned in a Strand 1 lesson and practiced in Strand 2 lessons.

At the beginning of the school year, particularly for kindergarten and first grade, teachers will have to perform all the roles played by students in a Strand 3 lesson several times before students will understand how to express their metacognitions and self-assessment thinking. Teacher modeling should continue until students understand how to describe their comprehension processes.

Objective of the Lesson

Students report how well they learned to infer and what they want to learn next to comprehend better.

Materials

Four to six students bring to a small-group meeting a story from a literature anthology or a trade book that they have read recently and enjoyed. Alternatively, sometimes the teacher or this group chooses to use the same text, and all students bring the same text to this small-group Strand 3.

Procedure

1. The teacher begins this Strand 3 lesson by asking students to put into words the thought processes they used to infer as they read the book

they brought to the circle. (The day before the Strand 3 lesson begins, the teacher asks students to bring the agreed upon book to this lesson and to have identified one or more points in that book in which they inferred.)

2. After the teacher describes how he or she inferred, the teacher asks the first student to describe the inference process in his or her language, and classmates ask how that student learned to do so or for the student to give suggestions as to how classmates can overcome a weakness in one of the steps in that comprehension process.

3. After the students answer his or her peers' questions, the teacher asks another student to read orally a page in his or her book where the student inferred and to tell the group how easy or difficult it was to infer at that point in the book and why.

4. This three-step process is then repeated several times, with the teacher asking other students to describe how they used (or learned) the inference comprehension process.

Conclusion

To support teachers' efforts in using research-based comprehension practices, administrators need knowledge concerning three types or strands of lessons that have proven to significantly increase primary-grade students' comprehension abilities. Strand 1 lessons provide teacher-directed, expanded explanations; comprehension motions; think-alouds; or thinking guides so students can learn new comprehension processes. Strand 2 lessons provide individualized mini-interventions for students when they are reading alone and have trouble comprehending. Strand 3 lessons teach students how to identify their comprehension strengths and weaknesses.

Principals and other administrators can use these lessons to (a) build a comprehension program, (b) assist individual teachers in increasing their students' comprehension abilities, and (c) form a foundation for assessing comprehension instruction when they observe it in classrooms. Teachers can use the information in these lessons to advance their skills in differentiating comprehension instruction. Most primary-grade students, particularly below-level readers, need the variety these lessons provide before they can become avid readers and independent comprehenders. All educators can use the information supplied in this chapter to assist them in their efforts to advance the reading abilities of all students. In doing so, every child may have the opportunity to come to love reading and use it as an important tool in his or her life, as Mr. Sullivan, the second-grade teacher described at the beginning of the chapter, demonstrated through his use of the CPI instructional cycle.

REFERENCES

Afflerbach, P. (2002). Teaching reading self-assessment strategies. In C.C. Block & M. Pressley (Eds.), *Comprehension instruction: Research-based best practices* (pp. 96–111). New York: Guilford.

Baker, L. (2002). Metacognition in comprehension instruction. In C.C. Block & M. Pressley (Eds.), *Comprehension instruction: Research-based best practices* (pp. 77–95). New York: Guilford.

Block, C.C. (1998, November). *New millennium reading.* Presentation to the Nobel Learning Communities' Biannual Board Meeting, Philadelphia.

Block, C.C. (1999). The case for exemplary teaching, especially for students who begin first grade without the precursors for literacy success. In T. Shanahan (Ed.), *49th yearbook of the National Reading Conference* (pp. 71–85). Chicago: National Reading Conference.

Block, C.C. (2000). *How can we teach all students to comprehend well?* (Research paper No. 4). New York: Scholastic.

Block, C.C. (2003). *Teaching comprehension: The comprehension process approach.* Boston: Allyn & Bacon.

Block, C.C. (in press). A research study of the effects of kinesthetic learning on below, on, and above grade level readings. *The Reading Teacher.*

Block, C.C., Gambrell, L.B., & Pressley, M. (Eds.). (2004). *Improving comprehension instruction: Rethinking research, theory, and classroom practice.* San Francisco: Jossey-Bass.

Block, C.C., & Israel, S. (2004). The ABCs of performing highly effective think-alouds. *The Reading Teacher, 58*(2), 154–167.

Block, C.C., & Johnson, R. (2002). The thinking process approach to comprehension development: Preparing students for their future comprehension challenges. In C.C. Block & M. Pressley (Eds.), *Comprehension instruction: Research-based best practices* (pp. 13–31). New York: Guilford.

Block, C.C., & Mangieri, J.N. (1995–1996). *Reason to read: Thinking strategies for life through literature* (Vols. 1, 2, & 3). Palo Alto, CA: Addison-Wesley.

Block, C.C., & Mangieri, J.N. (2003). *Exemplary literacy teachers: Promoting success for all children in grades K–5.* New York: Guilford.

Block, C.C., & Pressley, M. (Eds.). (2002). *Comprehension instruction: Research-based best practices.* New York: Guilford.

Block, C.C., Rodgers, L., & Johnson, R. (2004). *Comprehension process instruction: Creating reading success in grades K–3.* New York: Guilford.

Block, C.C., & Whiteley, C. (in press). *Developing K–3 students' comprehension abilities: Using comprehension motions.* Urbana, IL: Language Arts. (Available: C.C. Block, Texas Christian University, Ft. Worth, TX)

Cain-Thoreson, C., Lippman, M.Z., & McClendon-Magnuson, C. (1997). Windows on comprehension: Reading comprehension processes as revealed by two think-aloud procedures. *Journal of Educational Psychology, 89*(4), 579–590.

Chall, J. (1998). *Teaching children to read.* Cambridge, MA: Brookline.

Collins, C. (1991). Reading instruction that increases thinking abilities. *Journal of Reading, 34*(7), 510–516.

Durkin, D. (1978–1979). What classroom observations reveal about reading comprehension instruction. *Reading Research Quarterly, 14*(4), 481–533.

Harris, T.L., & Hodges, R.E. (1995). *The literacy dictionary: The vocabulary of reading and writing.* Newark, DE: International Reading Association.

Keene, E.O., & Zimmermann, S. (1997). *Mosaic of thought: Teaching comprehension in a reader's workshop.* Portsmouth, NH: Heinemann.

Kintsch, W. (1999, April). *Comprehension transfer model.* Paper presented at the annual meeting of the American Educational Research Association, New Orleans, LA.

National Institute of Child Health and Human Development (NICHD). (2000). *Report of the National Reading Panel. Teaching children to read: An evidence-based assessment of the scientific research literature on reading and its implications for reading instruction* (NIH Publication No. 00-4769). Washington, DC: U.S. Government Printing Office.

No Child Left Behind Act of 2001, Pub. L. No. 107-110, 115 Stat. 1425 (2002). Retrieved October 1, 2005, from http://edworkforce.house.gov/issues/107th/education/nclb/nclb.htm

Omanson, R., Warren, R., & Trabasso, T. (1978, April). *Comprehending text through strategies.* Paper presented at the annual meeting of the American Educational Research Association, New Orleans, LA.

Paris, S.G., Wasik, B.A., & Turner, J. (1991). Portfolio assessment for young readers. *The Reading Teacher, 44*(9), 680–682.

Pearson, P.D., & Fielding, L. (1991). Comprehension instruction. In P.D. Pearson, E. Barr, P. Mosenthal, & M. Kamil (Eds.), *Handbook of reading research* (Vol. 2, pp. 815–860). Mahwah, NJ: Erlbaum.

Pressley, M., & Afflerbach, P. (1995). *Verbal protocols of reading: The nature of constructively responsive reading.* Hillsdale, NJ: Erlbaum.

CHAPTER 7

Oral Language: A Strong Foundation for Literacy Instruction

Carrice Cummins and Margaret Taylor Stewart

TERRI, a very active student repeating second grade, has struggled with reading and writing. During her first three years in school, she worked with her teachers and paraprofessionals on phonemic awareness and phonics. She heard many stories read to her at school. She worked through basal programs and had extra tutoring from Title I paraprofessionals. Terri has an inquisitive mind, but she does not remember what she learns from one day to the next. During the first week, her new teacher looks for a way to help Terri make connections to print—trying to find a "hook" to help Terri remember. She quickly notices Terri's gift for telling stories and decides to build on that obvious strength.

> Teacher: Tell me something that you really like or something that you do well.
> Terri: I love to take care of my baby cousin, and I'm really good at it!
> Teacher: Would you like to make a picture book about taking care of your baby cousin? You could bring in photos and write about them.
> Terri: (Smiles sadly) Well, I would, but I have lots of trouble when I try to write words.
> Teacher: What if I act as your scribe (that's sort of like your secretary) and write it for you? Then we can work on reading it, so you can read it any time you want to. You will be the author and illustrator, and I will be your secretary until you're ready to do the writing yourself. (Cherry, 1995b, pp. 39–40)

Understanding and Implementing Reading First Initiatives: The Changing Role of Administrators by Carrice Cummins, Editor. Copyright © 2006 by the International Reading Association.

rom that point forward, Terri and her teacher squeezed times during the school day to work from Terri's oral language, using storytelling of events from Terri's life that were highly significant to her. Terri learned to connect the oral language she already knew with words and letters she was learning. Because the stories were important to her and because she wanted to share them with others, she worked hard and long to learn to read them. She posted her stories on the wall with other students' stories and used them as references when she wanted to spell. Learning to read her own words was the "way in" for Terri, who became a reader by the end of the year.

Why Emphasize Oral Language Instruction?

Language is power, and the effective use of language is powerful, as evidenced by Terri's literacy growth. Although oral language was not identified as one of the five essential elements of Reading First, a part of the No Child Left Behind Act of 2001 (2002), it is the foundation for strong literacy instruction. As previously mentioned, oral language was omitted from the findings of the National Reading Panel Report of 2000 (NRP; National Institute of Child Health and Human Development), not because it was unimportant, but because there was not enough time for the panel to study everything they considered important regarding reading and literacy. Oral language is mentioned sixth in a list of topics that the NRP considered but did not study (Shanahan, 2003). Other important studies place oral language much higher in priority (e.g., Dickinson & Snow, 1987; Hart & Risley, 1995; Purcell-Gates, 1988).

Longitudinal data collected by Hart and Risley (1995) show that children from low-income families hear dramatically fewer words at home during preschool years compared to children of professional parents. This large disparity in language experience is tightly linked to differences in child literacy outcomes. Some startling statistics from the study include the following:

- The more parents talked to their children, the faster the children's vocabularies grew and the higher the children's IQ test scores were at age 3 and later.
- There was a difference of almost 1,500 words spoken per hour between professional and welfare families. Extrapolating this verbal interaction to a year, a child in a professional family would hear 11 million words.

- In contrast, children from a welfare family who heard fewer than 500 words per hour could start kindergarten having heard 32 million fewer words than their wealthier classmates.
- It would take 41 hours per week of interacting in an out-of-the-home environment with language on the level of that of professional families to bring children of welfare families up to the language level of children of middle-class families.

Oral language is a large aspect of overall literacy and is an important aid to print literacy—both the acquisition and enhancement of it. It is a skill that educators often think "just happens" (is acquired naturally); however, the skill requires the same planned opportunities for development, degree of explicit modeling, and extensive time for practice as other skills. To be most productive, it really should occur within the context of other subjects in order to enhance content understanding while providing an opportunity to facilitate language use for authentic purposes. Oral language development not only helps students communicate effectively but also helps them with reading and writing.

Oral language instruction is an area in which administrators can and should play a key role in structuring support for teachers and students. Savvy administrators scaffold teacher inclusion of oral language instruction in the classroom. They understand the value of oral language, not as a separate subject, but as a foundational component that builds literacy skills, particularly those identified in Reading First as core components of reading (i.e., phonemic awareness, phonics, fluency, vocabulary, and reading comprehension). It is important for administrators to understand the role of oral language in literacy so they can be instrumental in helping teachers increase the emphasis on oral language instruction in the classroom and verbal communication throughout the school day.

Oral Language Instructional Strategies

The strategies of talk and daily read-alouds are only two of the strategies teachers can implement in their efforts to enhance oral language instruction in the classroom; however, they are two of the most powerful ones (e.g., Calkins, 2001; Campbell, 2001; Roskos, Tabors, & Lenhart, 2004). For explanatory purposes, we discuss these strategies as isolated entities. It is important to remember, however, that the most powerful oral language instruction occurs when these and other language-developing strategies are integrated throughout all aspects of the school day. This integration ensures that oral language instruction is used in purposeful and active ways while addressing two important goals: (1) communicating effectively and (2) scaffolding learners' reading, writing, and content knowledge.

Talk

The power of talk is often all that many children initially bring with them to the classroom, yet it is frequently one of the first things that some educators stifle. This is unfortunate because talk is the way that children "build their practical knowledge of language—the verbal system. This is how they learn new words and gain mastery of language rules. Children's language knowledge gained through talking becomes the basis for developing essential reading and writing skills" (Roskos et al., 2004, p. 9). Just as we know that the more children read, the better readers they become, we know that the more opportunities children have to talk, the better they are at using language effectively. In essence, one learns to talk by talking. However, Calkins (2001) states, "In schools, talk is sometimes valued and sometimes avoided, but—and this is surprising—talk is rarely taught.... Yet talk, like reading and writing, is a major motor—I could even say the major motor—of intellectual development" (p. 226).

Hart and Risley (1995) made a profound discovery regarding the overwhelming importance of talk in the home. They found that "the amount of experience children accumulate with parenting that provides language diversity, affirmative feedback, symbolic emphasis, gentle guidance, and responsiveness" (p. 210) is far more important than any material and educational advantages available in the home. Realizing the applicability of talk for schools, strong administrators and teachers should strive to create similar conditions in classrooms. Encouraging, engaging in, and responding to focused talk throughout the school day is an important and effective way teachers do this. They make sure that reading and writing float "on a sea of talk" (Britton, 1983).

Wise teachers and administrators realize that silent classrooms inhibit oral language development, so they model effective communication and set high expectations for children to purposefully interact throughout the day. When students make brief statements or answer questions with one or two words, effective teachers scaffold their students' language and understanding by

- allowing time for elaboration;
- eliciting more information;

- using facial expressions, body language, and words to demonstrate interest;
- refraining from using only comments that cut off conversation (e.g., not just "That's great!" or "Very good"); and
- asking more about what the speaker has to say (e.g., "How did you know to...?", "What makes you say that...?", "Tell me about....").

Administrators who model effective oral communication in their interactions with teachers and students elevate the level of language used in their schools—both the level of vocabulary and the level of communication. Successful teachers and administrators know how important it is for students to converse with master conversationalists (both adults and more proficient students) who raise the level of talk. They know it is the talk surrounding an activity, rather than the activity itself, that is most important for building oral language, enlarging vocabulary, extending knowledge, and scaffolding a sense of efficacy in learners. Administrators should encourage teachers to arrange desks and work spaces to accommodate talk, thus deliberately making working conversations a part of the classroom environment. Administrators also need to support teachers in their explicit instruction to help students talk with their partners or groups about their work and ideas. Having talk at the center of instruction is an important aspect of learning. Administrators who set the tone of acceptance and encouragement of "productive noise," rather than mandating silent classrooms and lunchrooms, promote literacy development at many levels.

Effective administrators encourage teachers to emphasize language at every opportunity. Beck, McKeown, and Kucan (2002) offer an example of a teacher engaging a student in productive talk. The following exchange took place in February in a high-poverty first-grade classroom of very struggling readers.

Jason: Is this going to be an ordinary day?

Ms. H: What would make it ordinary?

Jason: If we like did the same old thing.

Ms. H: What might make it not ordinary, make it exceptional?

Jason: If you gave us prizes for being good—I mean exceptional and mature. (p. 47)

In this everyday exchange between a teacher and student, the teacher took advantage of a teachable moment to extend the student's language. She could have replied to his question by saying offhandedly,

"Yes," and glossed over this opportunity. Instead, she took the extra moment or two to "ratchet up" the student's learning by not only asking him a question to probe his understanding of the word but also offering a nonexample to further push the child's vocabulary knowledge. This is similar to what Bruner (1978) described mothers doing to extend their children's language. This type of elaboration can and should be conducted by administrators as well as teachers.

The fact that this scene took place in February shows that such exchanges were common in this classroom. The child's response reveals his adeptness with language and his ability to immediately incorporate new vocabulary into his ordinary speech. This example shows how high-level talk is scaffolded, even in high-poverty classrooms with readers who are struggling with print. It is this level of conversation that builds literacy. It is not difficult, but it does require that teachers and administrators consistently model such strategies.

In addition to conversations that extend learning during activities, administrators should encourage teachers to conduct "grand conversations," as described by Peterson and Eeds (1990), in which students and teachers coproduce meaning as they take up one anothers' ideas, expand them, and add to them. Grand conversations are give-and-take discussions in which the partners in a dialogue depend on one another's patience, ideas, and encouragement. A grand conversation usually develops around a particular class theme. For example, a grand conversation could be in the form of a group inquiry session built around literature that the class has read or heard. An inquiry session typically proceeds as follows:

1. The teacher and students sit in a large circle, facing one another.

2. Participants explore the story they have read or heard by asking thoughtful, open-ended questions and discussing issues that could have more than one answer.

3. Students take a stance on an issue.

4. Students defend that stance based on personal beliefs, information from the story, and various other reasons.

An inquiry session builds language, flexibility of mind, and consideration of alternate viewpoints. The following example from a second-grade inquiry session about the fairy tale "Jack and the Beanstalk" shows students' comments concerning whether or not this was a good story for children.

Ranea: I don't think this story is good because it has stealing, lying, and killing in it. I don't think this should be in our class.

Tom: We can take the violence out of the book so that some other kids won't get an idea about killing other kids.

Shandra: I think that it is a bad story for the class. It has stealing and violence in it. But we can learn never to steal. I liked some of the story. I liked the part that Jack and his wife lived happily ever after.

Larry: I think this is a good thing to do in the class. We can really use our brains, and we can really work hard. We are having good questions and answers, too. Everybody likes to think about this in the classroom. On some things you have to use your big brain to answer some of the questions. And you have to read a lot, too! (Cherry, 1995a, p. 4)

Students who participate in inquiry sessions and other grand conversations experience many of the positive things that Galda, Cullinan, and Strickland (1993) mention when describing five qualities that usually surround oral language development at home. First, there is a warm, rewarding atmosphere in which children's utterances are received with pleasure and in which children are listened to as if they make sense. Second, development of language occurs within a social, child-centered context in which adults and peers accept children and their language as they talk *with* rather than *at* children. Third, language and conceptual development occur within meaningful contexts in which language is used purposefully as children experience and explore their world. Fourth, the entire language system is presented to children at once, not in tiny bits and pieces. Fifth, children learn the linguistic aspects of language or the "rules"—phonology (sounds), syntax (structure), and semantics (meaning)—while they learn how to use language (pragmatics) to communicate in various ways. Strong teachers provide similar qualities in their classrooms as they structure safe learning environments in which students are free to take risks by asking questions or giving responses, knowing that they will not be disparaged or embarrassed by the teacher or any of their fellow classmates. Students quickly learn that it is OK to discuss ideas, even if their ideas are different. They learn that they have the power to persuade, and they learn to be open-minded and analytical as they explore the ideas of their classmates and teacher. In addition to the improvement in language, respect, knowledge, and engagement are enhanced when classrooms (as previously mentioned) float on a sea of talk.

Read-Alouds

Reading aloud is one of the most influential factors in helping students become proficient readers (Bickart, Jablon, & Dodge, 1999; Leu & Kinzer, 1999; Trelease, 1995).

> Reading aloud to children improves their reading, writing, speaking, listening—and, best of all, their attitudes about reading.... If Americans are to manage in a more complicated world, our thinking must be deeper and more complicated. Nothing trains the mind as quickly and as thoroughly as reading. Reading is our life preserver. (Trelease, 1995, pp. xvii, 352)

The importance of this simple, yet highly engaging and motivational activity cannot be overemphasized because the benefits are numerous. Reading aloud to children, in general,

- provides a model for strong oral language,
- provides an understanding of how print works,
- builds vocabulary,
- develops knowledge of letters and letter–sound relations,
- develops a sense of story,
- develops understanding of story structure, and
- builds a positive attitude and love for books.

Specifically in the area of oral language development, books read aloud to children provide wonderful opportunities for them to

- hear rich language,
- develop an understanding of decontextualized or book language (language out of the here-and-now),
- develop a sense of how words are put together to form sentences, and
- become familiar with language patterns and structures.

The term *read-aloud*, as used here, refers to the concept of an adult's reading a book to a child or to a group of children (Trelease, 1995). Most teachers agree that reading aloud to children is important, yet many feel uncomfortable about devoting time to the activity. However, "few children learn to love books by themselves. Someone has to lure them into the wonderful world of the written word; someone has to show them the way" (Prescott, 1965, p. 13).

The enjoyment the children and teacher glean from the experience often makes the read-aloud seem like "play" rather than instruction (Routman, 1994; Short, 1999). It is this enjoyment that "forms the basis for learning about stories and reading, learning to read, learning through literacy, and wanting to read" (Campbell, 2001, p. 31). Thus, read-alouds should take place every day and be considered vital classroom instruction.

Planning an Interactive Read-Aloud

Most educators agree that children should be read to at least once daily; however, read-alouds may be carried out in different ways and for different purposes. A read-aloud can stand alone and be used strictly for relaxation and enjoyment; but when utilized for a more direct instructional purpose, it can serve as a springboard for numerous literacy activities. For example, "to facilitate understanding of how text works, teachers read books to their students that are chosen to highlight specific literary purposes: story elements, genres, skills, or language development" (Benson & Cummins, 2000, p. 37).

There are so many wonderful books available for reading aloud that teachers may be tempted to grab one haphazardly just before reading time. However, to reap the full benefits of a read-aloud, they need to pay more deliberate attention to the task. Wade (1990) states that "stories need to be introduced, presented, recommended, talked over, and savored together" (p. 31). In other words, teachers must prepare for a read-aloud as they would prepare for any other part of their instruction. Aspects to consider when planning for a basic read-aloud may vary if the read-aloud is being used to focus on a certain aspect of literacy development. For the purposes of this chapter, the interactive read-aloud is considered to be a planned instructional component focused on the enhancement of oral language development.

A recent study conducted by Fisher, Flood, Lapp, and Frey (2004) identified seven essential components for conducting an interactive read-aloud: (1) selecting appropriate texts, (2) previewing and practicing reading, (3) identifying purpose, (4) modeling fluent reading, (5) reading with expression, (6) stopping periodically to conduct specific oral discussions, and (7) making connections. The checklist in Figure 7.1 incorporates these and other components in a time frame of before, during, and after reading and highlights their impact as they relate more directly to oral language development.

• Figure 7.1 •
Interactive Read–Aloud Checklist

Before Reading
- ☐ Select text
- ☐ Preview and practice reading
- ☐ Identify purpose and/or focus
- ☐ Conduct oral discussions—focus skill and/or establish predictions

During Reading
- ☐ Model fluent reading
- ☐ Read with animation and expression
- ☐ Conduct oral discussion as needed to monitor meaning

After Reading
- ☐ Conduct oral discussion—focus skill, favorite parts, confirm or disconfirm earlier predictions, and so forth
- ☐ Make connections
- ☐ Conduct extension activities when needed or as appropriate (e.g., making lists, retelling the story, drawing, role playing, and so forth)

Before Reading

One of the most important aspects of preparing for a read-aloud is selecting the book. Teachers should base book selection first on student interest and second on the book's ability to highlight the chosen oral language skill. Teachers should preview and practice reading the book. This not only provides opportunities for the teacher to identify any areas of difficulty that might occur during the reading but also allows practice time so that the reading can be done with appropriate intonation and expression. Before reading, students also should be actively engaged in making predictions about the content of the text (via title, book cover, pictures, and so forth). This allows topic knowledge, which already exists for some students, to be brought to a conscious level and helps establish topic knowledge for other students. This activation of schemata before reading promotes a deeper understanding of text during reading.

During Reading

During an interactive read-aloud, the teacher fluently reads the book with zeal and enthusiasm. The level of the text and the interest level of the students should determine whether the book is read in its entirety or in sections. While students enjoy hearing the language of the text, they also must walk away with the "big picture" of what the author is attempting to say. Students often are able to do this simply by listening to the story, but sometimes they need to ask questions or interrupt with comments. Effective teachers invite their students to be active in the reading by pausing and having the students predict what will happen next. Although the most active dialogue about the story often occurs after the reading, the discussion that takes place *during* reading is extremely important in keeping students' comprehension on track. As students participate in interactive read-alouds, they not only learn how to make meaning from the text but also how to talk about it. Teachers must encourage students to confirm or disconfirm predictions made before and during the reading, as well as to share their feelings about the story. This sharing facilitates the establishment of connections and, as Trelease (1995) notes, it also allows time for students' thoughts, hopes, fears, and discoveries to surface.

After Reading

After-reading activities are designed to help students extend their learning and comprehension. Readers return to books because of the way they feel about the reading; therefore, after-reading extensions should be chosen based on students' abilities to validate their feelings about the book, model language to talk about the book, and provide structured and supportive opportunities to respond to the book. Combs (1996) shares the importance of teachers' valuing students' opinions about books and helping them find the words to talk about their interpretations of books because responding to literature enables students to think in creative and critical ways. Sketch to stretch, role playing, and retelling are only a few of the many activities that can be used to help students express their interpretations of text.

Sketch to Stretch. Sketch to stretch (Short, Harste, & Burke, 1995) is an extension activity in which students quickly draw a sketch that represents what the story means to them. Students show their sketches to the class and explain their interpretations of the story. The discussion can be extended to include a conversation about the different ideas the students had about the same story.

Role Play. Role playing is an excellent way to encourage dialogue about a story because students naturally use stories they have heard in their play activities at school. Role playing can be left entirely to the children or can include the teacher through various degrees of involvement (Campbell, 2001). The teacher can assist students in conducting a dramatized version of the story or simply prepare an area of the room and leave the children to role play together. A versatile and flexible structure for this activity is to have a pole added to each end of a bookcase. Across the top of the two poles, teachers can attach a rod on which a divided curtain can be hung so that a moveable "stage" is available for use as a puppet stage, a reception desk, a doctor's office, a principal's office, a grocery store, or other imaginative setting.

Retelling. Retelling is a form of dialogue that is a long-established part of our daily conversations—for example, "Tell me what you did last night" or "Now tell me what happened." When used to encourage dialogue about a story, it is probably one of the most comprehensive methods for developing oral language because it requires students to use a multitude of expressive verbal skills.

A retelling is not just a short-term recall of all that the child can remember from the story but rather is the child's construction of meaning (Benson & Cummins, 2000). The complexity of this task requires the teacher to scaffold the activity. Initially, the teacher models how to retell the stories and slowly invites the students to join in. Illustrations, story props, and graphic organizers should be used one at a time to support the person doing the retelling. The use of these items frees the students from trying to remember all of the details of the story so they can focus on the language needed to put the story in their own words. As students gain more experience, they can record their retellings using a tape recorder, write a retelling of a favorite piece of literature, or create a picture book retelling about a favorite experience (Stewart, 2002a, 2002b).

Figure 7.2 provides a simple template for planning the interactive read-aloud. Even though each time frame is designed to enhance the experience, it is important to remember that teachers should be cautious about doing too much with the book. Stopping too many times during the reading can interrupt the flow of the language, and too much discussion can reduce the enjoyment gained from the reading experience. The interactive read-aloud should be planned, organized, and well thought through; however, the text should not be pulled apart to the extent that enjoyment and meaning are jeopardized. Not every read-aloud should be conducted as an interactive activity because some books and/or reading opportunities simply lend themselves to having children sit back and listen to a wonderful story.

• Figure 7.2 •
Interactive Read–Aloud Template

Title:_____

Author:_____

Oral Language Focus: _____

_____

Before Reading: _____

_____

_____

_____

_____

During Reading: _____

_____

_____

_____

_____

After Reading:_____

_____

_____

_____

_____

As stated earlier, reading aloud is one of the most influential factors in helping students become proficient readers. It is a simple strategy requiring minimal time, and it also is a strategy that children love and that provides numerous opportunities for literacy development in general and oral language development specifically. This section has focused on the development of oral language through children's engagement in narrative text; however, it is important to note that expository text can also be used to develop oral language skills through read-alouds.

Read-alouds should always be enjoyable, but, when carefully crafted, they can also provide excellent opportunities for students to hear high-level language and practice using it, in addition to building other areas of literacy development. Sloan (1991) sums up the power of a good read-aloud: "[S]tory read-alouds provide the basis for children to learn about literacy, to become readers and writers, to learn through literacy, and to want to read in the future" (p. 6).

Conclusion

Administrators are currently in the throes of efforts to improve reading achievement through increased emphasis on phonemic awareness, phonics, vocabulary, fluency, and comprehension. All of these elements identified by the NRP are essential in reading instruction; however, each element requires a foundational skill to be in place. Oral language development is that foundational skill because it underlies future success in reading and writing. Children who do not posses strong oral language skills in their early years find it difficult to keep pace with their peers, and they start to fall behind (Snow, Burns, & Griffin, 1998).

Purposeful and active engagement in oral language activities helps children learn the language system and ways to use it to express their own ideas, interpret the ideas of others, or both. An understanding of children's oral language development is particularly important to administrators, as they often set the tone for the "noise level" of the school. Administrators can help teachers understand the power of oral language and the role it plays in reading and writing. Once this understanding is in place, teachers can provide numerous opportunities for students to participate in activities that strengthen the development of oral language. Daily talks and interactive read-alouds are only two of many strong components of a sound oral language development program. Administrators can make a difference by talking to and with teachers and children and by encouraging teachers to make constructive talk and daily read-alouds an integral part of the K–3 instructional program.

REFERENCES

Beck, I.L., McKeown, M.G., & Kucan, L. (2002). *Bringing words to life: Robust vocabulary instruction*. New York: Guilford.

Benson, V., & Cummins, C. (2000). *The power of retelling: Developmental steps for building comprehension.* Bothell, WA: Wright Group McGraw-Hill.

Bickart, T.S., Jablon, J.R., & Dodge, D.T. (1999). *Building the primary classroom: A complete guide to teaching and learning.* Washington, DC: Teaching Strategies; Portsmouth, NH: Heinemann.

Britton, J. (1983). Writing and the story world. In B. Kroll & G. Wells (Eds.), *Explorations in the development of writing: Theory, research, and practice* (pp. 3–30). New York: Wiley.

Bruner, J.S. (1978). The role of dialogue in language acquisition. In A. Sinclair, R.J. Jarvella, & W.J.M. Levelt (Eds.), *The child's conception of language* (pp. 241–256). Berlin, Germany: Springer-Verlag.

Calkins, L.M. (2001). *The art of teaching reading.* Toronto, ON: Addison Wesley.

Campbell, R. (2001). *Read-alouds with young children.* Newark, DE: International Reading Association.

Cherry, M.T. (1995a). [Class big book, Jack and the beanstalk]. Unpublished raw data.

Cherry, M.T. (1995b). [Fieldnotes from elementary setting]. Unpublished raw data.

Combs, M. (1996). *Developing competent readers and writers in the primary grades.* Englewood Cliffs, NJ: Merrill-Prentice Hall.

Dickinson, D.K., & Snow, C.E. (1987). Interrelationships among prereading and oral language skills in kindergartners from two social classes. *Early Childhood Research Quarterly, 2*(1), 1–25.

Fisher, D., Flood, J., Lapp, D., & Frey, N. (2004). Interactive read-alouds: Is there a common set of implementation practices? *The Reading Teacher, 58*(1), 8–17.

Galda, L., Cullinan, B.E., & Strickland, D.S. (1993). *Language, literacy, and the child* (2nd ed.). Fort Worth, TX: Harcourt Brace Jovanovich College.

Hart, B., & Risley, T.R. (1995). Meaningful differences in the everyday experience of young American children. Baltimore: Paul H. Brookes.

Leu, D.J., & Kinzer, C.K. (1999). *Effective literacy instruction, K–8* (4th ed.). Upper Saddle River, NJ: Merrill.

National Institute of Child Health and Human Development. (2000). *Report of the National Reading Panel. Teaching children to read: An evidence-based assessment of the scientific research literature on reading and its implications for reading instruction* (NIH Publication No. 00-4769). Washington, DC: U.S. Government Printing Office.

No Child Left Behind Act of 2001, Pub. L. No. 107-110, 115 Stat. 1425 (2002). Retrieved October 1, 2005, from http://edworkforce.house.gov/issues/107th/education/nclb/nclb.htm

Peterson, R.I., & Eeds, M. (1990). *Grand conversations.* New York: Scholastic.

Prescott, O. (Ed.). (1965). *A father reads to his children: An anthology of prose and poetry.* New York: E.P. Dutton.

Purcell-Gates, V. (1988). Lexical and syntactic knowledge of written narrative held by well-read-to kindergartners and second graders. *Research in the Teaching of English, 22,* 128–160.

Roskos, K.A., Tabors, P.O., & Lenhart, L.A. (2004). *Oral language and early literacy in preschool.* Newark, DE: International Reading Association.

Routman, R. (1994). *Invitations: Changing as teachers and learners K–12.* Portsmouth, NH: Heinemann.

Shanahan, T. (2003). Research-based reading instruction: Myths about the National Reading Panel report. *The Reading Teacher, 56*(7), 646–657.

Short, J.C., Harste, K.G., & Burke, C. (1995). *Creating classrooms for authors and inquirers* (2nd ed.). Portsmouth, NH: Heinemann.

Short, K. (1999). The search for "balance" in literacy instruction. *English in Education, 33*(3), 43–53.

Sloan, G.D. (1991). *The child as critic: Teaching literature in elementary and middle schools* (3rd ed.). New York: Teachers College Press.

Snow, C.E., Burns, M.S., & Griffin, P. (Eds.). (1998). *Preventing reading difficulties in young children*. Washington, DC: National Academy Press.

Stewart, M.T. (2002a). *"Best practice"? Insights on literacy instruction from an elementary classroom*. Newark, DE: International Reading Association; Chicago: National Reading Conference.

Stewart, M.T. (2002b). *Writing: It's in the bag! Inspiring young children to write*. Peterboro, NH: Crystal Springs.

Trelease, J. (1995). *The read-aloud handbook* (4th ed.). New York: Penguin.

Wade, B. (Ed.). (1990). *Reading for real*. Buckingham, England: Open University Press.

CHAPTER 8

Where Does Writing Fit in Reading First?

Timothy Shanahan

MR. JANSEN, the school principal, is alarmed when he enters Mrs. Ames's third-grade classroom during reading/language arts because he finds all the students at their desks writing and Mrs. Ames circulating around the room conferring with individual children about their compositions. Mr. Jansen is concerned because his school receives Reading First funding, and Reading First does not emphasize the teaching of writing. If Mrs. Ames is spending time teaching "unnecessary" aspects of the language arts, maybe the school would fail to make adequate yearly progress; maybe they even would lose their Reading First funding. Mr. Jansen wonders if he should order Mrs. Ames to stop teaching writing for the time being. Should he ask that she devote that time to the key elements (phonemic awareness, phonics, oral reading fluency, vocabulary, and comprehension) of Reading First?

Reading First has its basis in the work of the National Reading Panel Report of 2000 (NRP; National Institute of Child Health and Human Development [NICHD]). The five elements that are stressed in the law are those aspects of teaching for which NRP found sol-

Understanding and Implementing Reading First Initiatives: The Changing Role of Administrators by Carrice Cummins, Editor. Copyright © 2006 by the International Reading Association.

id, supporting research evidence that instruction in each of those elements gave students a clear learning advantage. Consequently, the U.S. government provides money for materials, assessments, professional development, and help for struggling readers, but only in the five elements. The idea is that, although there might be other good things to do with students, spending this money solely on what is certain to help students learn would be a good start toward raising reading achievement.

But what about writing? NRP identified writing as one of approximately 30 potentially important topics to explore, but they did not have enough time to review it; therefore, writing is not yet eligible for Reading First support. However, writing is valuable—both because writing is useful in its own right, and because writing instruction has been shown under some circumstances to improve reading achievement (Shanahan, in press; Tierney & Shanahan, 1991). Writing still needs to be taught, but such instruction must proceed with state and local support alone—just as schools must continue to teach math, science, and social studies although no federal support is provided for these subjects through Reading First. The following three instructional activities illustrative of the types of composition that should be going on in primary-grade classes—activities that can help students to do better in both writing and reading.

Defining Writing Instruction

Writing Marathons

Perhaps no aspect of writing is as challenging for young students as "elaboration," that aspect of writing that describes a sufficiency of information and a degree of fluent writing—that is, students need to learn to communicate a sufficient amount of information with some speed and ease (Berninger, Abbott, Abbott, Graham, & Richards, 2002). Young children struggle to get their ideas on paper because forming letters can be difficult for them and spelling stands in their way even longer. Students get into the early habit of not telling much in their writing, and then this terse quality may persist—often leaving teachers surprised and disappointed when they see the meager results from their latest writing assignment.

The writing marathon, or nonstop paper, can be a good way to obtain a substantial amount of writing in a short time (Shanahan, 1977). Of course, quality is an issue too, but initially elaboration and fluency should be emphasized because without these elements students are not able to develop quality compositions (Berninger et al., 2002). Once students can easily put their thoughts into writing, there is plenty of time to guide other improvements, but it is difficult to try to revise a paper with little content.

How does a writing marathon work? Teachers begin by telling students what a marathon is—a long-distance run or race requiring concentrated effort. The teacher might tell them about Phidippides, who ran from Marathon to Athens to warn the Greeks of a coming invasion, or talk about the Olympics's marathon or a local one. Students can use this definition as a basis for understanding writing marathons. Just like the running marathons, a writing marathon is a sustained event and requires concentrated effort—nothing goes on during a writing marathon except writing.

It also is important that students get started with the right equipment. Students need paper and pencils, and extra supplies should be ready to keep them on track. Then, teachers should present students with the rules:

- When the marathon begins, nothing can be done except writing—all the way to the end.
- If a student runs out of paper or breaks a pencil, he or she should raise a hand so the teacher can replace it.
- If a student runs out of ideas, he or she should rewrite the last complete sentence (no running out of ideas just to rest weary fingers).
- If a student is uncertain how to spell a word, he or she should do his or her best and plan to fix it later because there is no time to stop for spelling.

Finally, the teacher presents the writing topic and the teacher and students discuss the idea for a few minutes to make sure they have something to help them get started.

After presenting the rules, it is time to begin. (I chant, "Ready, set, go.") The students usually start fast, but some soon falter. The teacher must urge them on like an excited race observer. There often is laughter and even some talking, but everybody writes. For a while, they write fast, which is fine, but later they figure out that they can slow down and still keep writing. The teacher might want to avoid telling the students how long a marathon will be to help discourage them from watching the clock. First graders might begin with a one-minute marathon (even a half minute), and this might be stretched to 2–3 minutes for beginning third graders.

After they have done this quick piece of writing (which usually is no longer than what they normally write and sometimes is shorter), the teacher should prepare them for a second and even a third marathon. These subsequent marathons might be a bit longer, never more than 2–3 minutes with first graders, and even that time length must be built up to, and never more than 5–6 minutes with third graders. After each marathon, students need to stretch and rest their tired hands. During the pause, the teacher should allow time for students to share their papers aloud, if desired.

The final step in this activity is to have each student revise his or her paper into something complete and finished—which nearly everyone gladly does given that these papers are usually incomplete, sometimes have repeated sentences, and are messy. The teacher might sometimes have them finish their "best" piece of writing from a writing marathon or even combine all of such writings into a single piece. By the end, students should have written more elaborate first drafts than usual; and over time, from this kind of exercise, they should be able to produce writing more fluently and to elaborate. (The teacher can hold some marathon coaching sessions along the way about how to have enough to say, such as writing about each part of something or trying to tell two things about each idea introduced.)

Writing Complete Narratives With Story Maps

Of course, young students can write a lot, but they usually never tell a complete story. Completeness—having a beginning, middle, and end—is important in writing, and story maps can be a great way to introduce this idea to young children. Story maps are often used to teach reading (in fact, the NRP report of 2000 [NICHD] indicated a large number of studies with consistently positive findings supporting the impact of story mapping on reading comprehension), but they are just as useful in beginning writing.

Story maps are structural representations of the parts of a story. The simplest stories usually have a setting that tells when and where the story takes place, and they include a main character. The character usually has a goal to accomplish or some kind of problem to solve, and the story shows what the character does to make this happen. Finally, there is an outcome: The character succeeds or fails. When students get adept with this structure, the teacher can introduce more complex elements such as conflict, motivation, or psychological consequences, which are initially difficult for young children.

When explaining the parts of a story, it can be helpful for teachers to use a map or chart to physically represent the parts (see Figure 8.1).

• Figure 8.1 •
Story Map

Setting	Where and when does the story take place?
	In the woods
Character	Who has the goal or problems?
	Gretel
Goal/Problem	What is the goal? What is the problem?
	She wants to keep the witch from eating Hansel.
Solution	What does the character do?
	She shows Hansel how to fool the witch into thinking that he is skinny.

To introduce the idea of the map, I share a brief story with the children and match up the parts of the story with the map. It is best to start with a simple tale—simple in that there is only one main character, one problem, and not too much information about any one of the parts. Books like *Harold and the Purple Crayon* (Johnson, 1955) or *The Carrot Seed* (Krauss, 1974) are ideal for this purpose. The teacher can briefly summarize the information from the story on the map to show how it works.

Once students have the idea that stories have these parts, then the teacher can show how to apply this idea to writing. The teacher should start by having the class write a story as a group and then initiate discussion by reviewing the story maps and some story map questions. The first question might be, "Who will your story be about?" or "Who will have a problem?" The teacher should allow the students to tell who they want to write about. It can be someone real, including themselves, or it can be a made-up character, an animal, or an imaginary creature.

Then the teacher should ask, "What is the problem that your character is going to have?" This is a more difficult question, so it is helpful to get lots of ideas of possible problems from the class. Maybe the character loses something, or he or she gets lost. Maybe the character wants something badly but cannot have it for some reason. In the discussion, the teacher should ask several students to elaborate on possible solutions for a couple of the problems. Then, it is time to write. Students can use the story maps as planning tools to help them create their complete stories.

From Charts to Summaries

One of the most difficult things for students to do well—but one of the most worthwhile to learn—is how to write a good summary. (The NRP found that summarization instruction is one of the most powerful ways to improve reading comprehension.) A summary is just a shorter version of the essential information in a text or from an experience. To write a good summary, it is necessary to leave unnecessary information out, to delete what is repeated, and to replace lists of information with generalizations. Teaching students to summarize stories can be relatively easy because they can use story maps to strip stories down to their essential parts—omitting information that is not important. These completed story maps can be translated into paragraph form with relative ease.

But how can teachers teach students to summarize from expository texts such as science books or social studies passages? Probably the best way to start is with a content map. Content maps, like story maps, guide students to select the essential information and omit the rest. They provide a graphic synopsis of the text in a single page. Although the goal is to help students compose good summaries in writing, these kinds of graphics can be helpful. Unfortunately, because the organizational structures of expository text vary so much, it is impossible to recommend a single format for these graphics. For example, if a text makes a comparison, then it might be a good idea to use a Venn diagram with its interlocking circles (see Figure 8.2). Students fill in the Venn diagram by recording shared characteristics in the joint ring and contrasting features in the appropriate outer rings. Teachers should do a few diagrams with the students before having them try it alone or in small groups. There are many other charts that can be used to summarize text as well, including hierarchical maps for summarizing relations among concepts. For example, Figure 8.3 shows how the major ideas from an article on transportation fit together. "Transportation" (Oshiro, 1989) has two major sections: one on different ways to travel and one about new forms of transportation. In

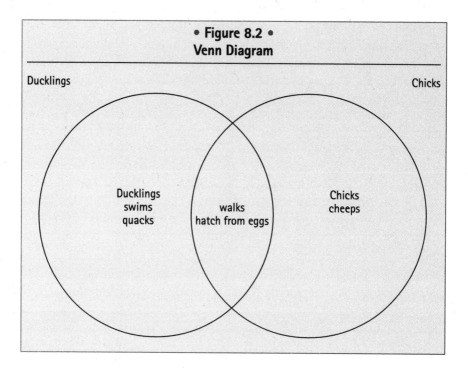

• Figure 8.2 •
Venn Diagram

Ducklings

Chicks

Ducklings
swims
quacks

walks
hatch from eggs

Chicks
cheeps

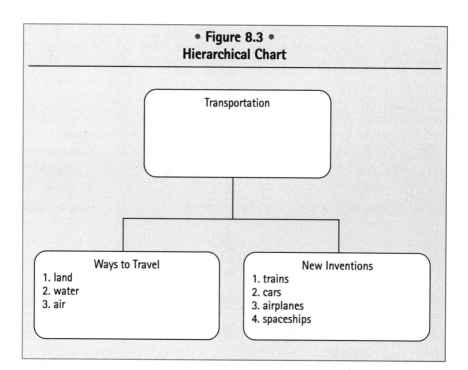

• Figure 8.3 •
Hierarchical Chart

Transportation

Ways to Travel
1. land
2. water
3. air

New Inventions
1. trains
2. cars
3. airplanes
4. spaceships

addition, two-column charts are great for summarizing cause-and-effect or problem–solution information.

Once students are adept at identifying key information in texts and translating that into the chart format, they are ready to try writing their own summaries. This is more difficult than completing a chart, though, because students cannot just fill in blanks. Therefore, the teacher should begin this kind of activity with a lot of modeling and whole-class work. The teacher should explain the value of summaries and then write a summary based on the students' charts. For example, Figure 8.4 includes a summary based on Figure 8.3. Some of the information in the summary came directly from the chart and is simply in sentence form. However, there is a need to include some other connecting or explanatory information that usually does not fit well into these charts. In this example, it was important to define transportation and tell why the article was talking about inventions, so additional facts about the article had to be included. Recording the summary in a two-column format (or using different colored markers for the different sentences) allows the teacher to show children where the different information came from. After completing a few summaries together, teachers can put students in small groups and have them create their own. Then, the summaries can be edited by the whole class to make sure they are clear, and that important facts are not omitted and extraneous information is not included. In time, students will be able to write summaries independently with little trouble.

• Figure 8.4 •
Summary Chart

Summary	Where It Came From
This article was about transportation.	Top box in the graph.
Transportation is how people get from place to place.	I included this because I thought it was a good idea to define what transportation is.
It told about three ways to travel: (1) land, (2) water, and (3) air.	Second box in the graph.
It said inventions change how we travel.	Header of second box in graph.
It told about four transportation inventions: (1) trains, (2) cars, (3) airplanes, and (4) spaceships.	Third box in the graph.

Conclusion

It is important to stress the teaching of writing in a school—not just because writing is valuable, but because writing activities such as the ones described in this chapter can help improve reading achievement. Research findings suggest that, under some circumstances, writing improves reading achievement (Tierney & Shanahan, 1991), and some of the findings of the NRP are encouraging with regard to the types of writing activities described here.

In addition, the NRP (NICHD, 2000) found that the practice provided by invented spelling helped students to develop phonemic awareness and phonics skills. Writing marathons create a great opportunity for purposeful practice of this type. (Students never balk at inventing spellings in this situation, and they do not have time to puzzle out how to keep from using words they do not know how to spell.) Although the NRP did not look directly at writing, it did consider the impact of teaching story maps in the context of reading and found evidence that such mapping led to higher reading comprehension. Finally, no single comprehension strategy had a bigger reading impact—or more research evidence—than summarization. If teachers perceive story maps and summaries as writing activities as much as reading activities, this perception may spur them to provide even more instruction and varied practice in these useful approaches in ways that can mutually benefit reading and writing.

REFERENCES

Berninger, V.W., Abbott, R.D., Abbott, S.P., Graham, S., & Richards, T. (2002). Writing and reading: Connections between language by hand and language by eye. *Journal of Learning Disabilities, 35*(1), 39–56.

National Institute of Child Health and Human Development (NICHD). (2000). *Report of the National Reading Panel. Teaching children to read: An evidence-based assessment of the scientific research literature on reading and its implications for reading instruction* (NIH Publication No. 00-4769). Washington, DC: U.S. Government Printing Office.

Shanahan, T. (1977). Writing marathons and concept development. *Language Arts, 54*, 403–405.

Shanahan, T. (in press). Relations among oral language, reading, and writing development. In C.A. MacArthur, S. Graham, & J. Fitzgerald (Eds.), *Handbook of writing research*. New York: Guilford.

Tierney, R.J., & Shanahan, T. (1991). Research on the reading–writing relationship: Interactions, transactions, and outcomes. In R. Barr, M.L. Kamil, P. Mosenthal, & P.D. Pearson (Eds.), *Handbook of reading research* (Vol. 2, pp. 246–280). Mahwah, NJ: Erlbaum.

LITERATURE CITED

Johnson, C. (1955). *Harold and the purple crayon*. New York: HarperCollins.

Krauss, R. (1974). *The carrot seed*. New York: HarperTrophy.

Oshiro, M. (1989). Transportation. In E. Sulzby, J. Hoffman, J. Niles, T. Shanahan, & W.H. Teale (Eds.), *Watch the wind* (pp. 104–108). New York: McGraw-Hill.

CHAPTER 9

Supporting Students' Motivation to Read

Jacquelynn A. Malloy, Linda B. Gambrell, and Gwendolyn Smith Williams

DEAR MRS. DAY,

Nancy found out who did it. It was Etienne did it. They can't figure out who the other kidnapper is. They think it is Tom because he always takes pictures of her wherever she is. He also works there so he knows the lights. So he could have cut them. I think Tom did it since every time he asks Bess for a date she would turn him down. Now he is getting back at Bess. Well Mrs. Day, this is my favorite book I have ever read in my whole life. I am even reading at home. My mom said you must be a very good teacher if you got me into reading. She can't believe it. When other teachers had me read I just sat there. So that is why she said that.

Sincerely,
Shannon

ost classroom teachers can readily identify students who are motivated to read. These are the students who have not only developed strong reading habits but who also find reading to be a rewarding and valuable activity. Alternately, teachers also can readily identify students who have become frustrated with reading because these students do not often choose to engage in reading and may even actively avoid it. Consequently, one of the most exciting things that can be observed in any classroom is the metamorphosis of a reluctant reader into a highly motivated one.

Consider the case of Shannon, an upper elementary grade struggling reader who made such a transformation after receiving the appropriate opportunities, resources, and support. Mrs. Day, the teacher in this classroom, provided time each day for students to read books of their own choosing and to write in their journals about the books they were reading. During journal-writing time, one of the activities in which they could participate was the Student-to-Teacher Reader Response Journal, an option that a majority of students favored. The teacher encouraged students to write letters to her in their journals about what they liked or disliked about the books they were reading and to describe the characters in the stories or the important ideas learned from informational text.

Shannon's letter to Mrs. Day paints a vivid portrait of a student who has progressed from being an admittedly disengaged reader to one who views herself as an engaged, motivated reader who is "into reading." As Shannon so aptly puts it, far too many students in our classrooms "just sit there" when they are reading. These are the students that educators worry about most, and with good reason; these students far too often become struggling readers who lack the literacy skills necessary to succeed in school.

The Reading First initiative, a part of the No Child Left Behind Act of 2001 (2002), as well as research compiled by the National Reading Panel (National Institute of Child Health and Human Development, 2000) encourages schools to focus quality instruction in the five key instructional areas addressed in this volume, and administrators can set the course for such instruction to be implemented. We assert, however, that it is also incumbent upon educational leaders to promote and support classroom cultures that encourage and nurture a motivation to read. School and classroom cultures that are strongly grounded in a motivation to read provide the necessary foundation for reading programs that support students' competence in the key instructional areas of phonemic awareness, phonics, vocabulary, fluency, and comprehension.

The Importance of Reading Motivation in the Reading Curriculum

Ask young children entering kindergarten why they need to go to school and they will invariably say, "So that I can learn to read and write." Young children, having become increasingly aware of print in their environment—and having noticed that "big kids" and "grown-ups" have managed some sort of access to this code—are strongly motivated by the "need to read." It is to them a rite of passage that will allow them to progress from emerging readers to proficient readers.

In kindergarten and first grade, children either become pleased or frustrated with the rate with which they acquire literacy skills, and depending on their success with "breaking the alphabetic code," come to see themselves as readers or failures. If the entire learning-to-read process becomes either frustratingly difficult or pointlessly boring, there will eventually be nothing left to sustain a child's interest in reading.

But consider what could happen if reading instruction were situated in a school and home culture where reading was valued. Imagine a classroom where students are eager to master more and better tools for reading and are excited about sharing book experiences because they want to read more challenging materials. Envision students who value reading as a source of pleasure, an avenue to investigating topics, and a means to solving problems and creating new works for others to use and enjoy. If students are not sufficiently motivated to become readers, they will not be adequately engaged in learning to read, and the very best instruction in phonemic awareness, phonics, vocabulary, fluency, and comprehension will not be sufficient to help them to become proficient, independent, lifelong readers.

The Expectancy–Value Theory of Motivation

The expectancy–value theory of motivation is particularly applicable to reading engagement (Pekrun, 1993; Wigfield & Eccles, 2000). According to this theory, the motivation to engage in a behavior is the product of the degree to which students expect to be able to perform the given task successfully and the degree to which they value the process of engaging in the task. In the case of literacy, students' motivation to read is a result of the self-perception that they are capable and competent with respect to reading activities (expectancy) as well as their recognition and appreciation of the value of the reading process. It becomes obvious that if the student perceives either the expectancy or the value to be low, there is a decreased likelihood that the student will actively engage in the reading activity. Alternately, students who perceive reading as having a high value and who expect that they will be successful in reading exhibit an increased likelihood of becoming engaged in the activity. Students do not willingly invest effort in tasks that they do not find enjoyable and that do not lead to outcomes that are valued; therefore, teachers need to be very intentional in helping students recognize and appreciate the value of reading and to ensure that students have successful reading experiences within the social context of the classroom (Brophy, 2004).

In a perfect world, this motivation would progress naturally. As children enter kindergarten, they typically place a very high value on learning to read and see it as a mastery goal that will lead them through to "grown-up" achievements. As long as their school and home environments mirror a value of reading and learning to read as a lifelong endeavor, this element should remain stable. However, when students experience difficulties in learning to read, whether because of a delay in skill development or possible learning problems, their perceived success (expectancy) in carrying out the learning-to-read process can plummet. In addition, if students' experiences with reading are unauthentic, uninteresting, and repetitively mundane, their perception of the value of reading will be undermined and drastically reduced. Consequently, it is important that teachers continue to place a high value on students becoming real-world readers with enjoyable and authentic experiences at school and at home. Learning to read should progress for each child from one success to another, with activities that provide obvious connections to their personal goals of reading to share and reading to learn.

Questions to Guide Administrators in Supporting Reading Motivation

Current research and descriptions of best practices in reading instruction suggest that students are more likely to become effectively engaged in literacy activities when they are (a) presented with authentic activities that access their prior knowledge and connect them to their home cultures (Brophy, 2004; Cunningham & Allington, 1999; Maehr, 1984); (b) actively involved in meaningful experiences that support student choice and goal setting (Cambourne, 1995; Guthrie & Wigfield, 1997; Schunk, 1998; Schunk & Zimmerman, 1997); and (c) afforded an environment that provides the necessary models, support, time, and materials necessary for literacy learning to flourish (Anderman & Midgley, 1992; Bandura, Barbaranelli, Caprara, & Pastorelli, 1996). Students' level of motivation will be influenced, for better or worse, by the culture of the classroom. With these ideas in mind, administrators can use the following five questions to assess aspects of classroom cultures that support and nurture reading motivation. When observing classrooms, it is helpful for administrators to consider the following:

1. Is the classroom rich in reading materials?
2. Are students provided with opportunities to choose the books they read?
3. Are students supported in learning how to choose appropriate-level books for self-selected reading?
4. Is adequate time allotted during the school day for independent reading?
5. Is time devoted to teachers sharing books with students and students sharing books with each other?

An understanding of the elements that cultivate motivating classrooms can assist administrators and teachers in fostering a love of reading for all students—those who are clearly motivated to read as well as those who are less so.

Is the Classroom Rich in Reading Materials?

Classrooms that provide an abundance and variety of reading materials for children support engagement with reading. A number of studies document that when classroom environments are rich in reading materials, the motivation to read is high (Allington & McGill-Franzen, 1993; Gambrell, 1993; Morrow, 1992; Neuman & Celano, 2001). These studies clearly suggest that increasing the number of books available to children in the classroom has a positive effect on the amount and quality of the literacy experiences in the classroom. Reutzel and Cooter (2004) recommend a minimum of three books for each student in the classroom, while the International Reading Association (2000) recommends seven books per student.

Students also need to be provided with a wide range of narrative and informational materials that reflect their interests and preferences. A classroom that is print-rich includes not only narrative and expository text but also poetry, magazines, and newspapers. This variety reflects authentic forms of text and communicates that reading is a worthwhile and valuable activity. Further, these types of classroom environments set the stage for students to develop the reading habit. It is evident that access to books is a significant factor in literacy development and that high-quality classroom libraries should be a priority.

Are Students Provided With Opportunities to Choose the Books They Read?

Providing a print-rich classroom is important, but not sufficient, to ensure that the classroom environment supports motivation to read. Students also need opportunities to read books of their own choosing to develop reading fluency and the reading habit. In a study of reading motivation, first-, third-, and fifth-grade students were asked to describe the books that they most enjoyed reading (Gambrell, 1996). Over 80% of the children interviewed in this study talked about books they had self-selected from their classroom libraries. Research by Spaulding (1992) and Schiefele (1991) supports the finding that the books students find most interesting and enjoyable to read are those they have selected for their own reasons and purposes. According to Schiefele, students who were allowed and encouraged to choose their own reading material expended more effort in learning and a gained a greater understanding of the material.

Are Students Supported in Learning How to Choose Appropriate-Level Books for Self-Selected Reading?

Students become more fluent and proficient readers when they have ample practice reading materials that are at the appropriate level— books that are neither too easy nor too difficult. During the primary grades, struggling readers who have difficulty in decoding begin to have less exposure to text than do more proficient readers (Allington, 1991; Gambrell, Wilson, & Gantt, 1981). According to Cunningham and Stanovich (1998), the lack of exposure and effective practice that results when there is a disparity between reading ability and reading level further impedes the development of fluency and word recognition skills, thus hindering reading comprehension.

Teachers can support students in learning to choose appropriate-level materials for self-selected reading by having students take responsibility for determining the levels of the books they choose. In elementary classrooms, it is important to talk with students about the fact that we all read easy, challenging, and difficult books at one time or another. However, the most progress in learning to read occurs when the books are challenging but not too difficult. Similar to "Goldilocks and the Three Bears," sometimes the porridge is "too hot," sometimes it is "too cold," but sometimes it is "just right." Teaching students simple strategies, such as reading a few pages from the middle of a book, can help them to determine whether the book is likely to be at an appropriate level for them. Although books that are too easy or difficult should not be denied them (especially if the topic is of particular interest), students need to be encouraged to spend most of their time reading books that are "just right." Students can also keep a log of the books they read to assist them in determining if most of their time is spent reading books at the most appropriate level for progress to occur.

Is Adequate Time Allotted During the School Day for Independent Reading?

Time should be devoted on a daily basis for independent, self-selected reading to provide students with the practice required to become fluent and proficient readers. Over the past three decades, a number of studies have documented that the *amount* of time spent reading is the major contributor to increased vocabulary development and reading proficiency (Allington, 1991; Allington & McGill-Franzen, 2003; Hayes & Ahrens, 1988; Nagy & Anderson, 1984; Stanovich, 1986; Taylor, Frye, & Maruyama, 1990). Providing sufficient time for reading yields dividends for all students, but struggling readers benefit most when time for reading is increased (Cunningham & Stanovich, 1998).

According to Cunningham and Stanovich (1998), reading has benefits that go beyond simply deriving meaning from text. Their research indicates that children who get off to a good start in reading are likely to read more as they progress through the grades. In addition, they contend that the very act of reading can help children compensate for modest levels of cognitive ability by increasing vocabulary and general knowledge. This research suggests that children who spend significant amounts of time reading improve their verbal intelligence and reading fluency.

How much time spent reading is necessary for students to become proficient readers? Although the research does not yield a definitive answer to this question, there are studies that provide some insight. In a study of teacher-guided reading, Gambrell (1986) found that students in first-, second-, and third-grade classrooms spent an average of only 3–5 minutes actually engaged in reading during the typical 30-minute teacher-directed reading lesson. This finding suggests that providing independent reading time during the school day may be critical to giving students the amount of practice needed for them to develop reading fluency and proficiency.

Is Time Devoted to Teacher Read-Alouds and Student Book Sharing?

Researchers sometimes ask students, "What motivates you to read?" One of the most frequently occurring responses is, "My teacher read this book (or part of this book) aloud to the class" (Artley, 1975; Palmer, Codling, & Gambrell, 1994). Reading aloud high-interest, high-quality literature to the class is a powerful motivational tool. When teachers read books and other materials to students, the children are often eager to get their hands on them.

Teacher read-aloud sessions can take a number of forms. Many teachers plan a specific time each day to read aloud to their students from high-interest, high-quality children's literature. Another effective technique is for the teacher to introduce and read short segments from three or four books each day. For example, the teacher might introduce and read a brief portion from a narrative book, an informational book, and a book of poetry. The teacher would then tell the students that they might like to try one of these books during their independent reading time. In this way, book-sharing techniques help children become familiar and comfortable with a range of texts.

In addition, there is ample evidence that talking with others about books has a positive influence on reading motivation and achievement (Almasi, 1995; McCombs, 1989; Oldfather, 1993). Students who have opportunities to talk about what they have read with friends and family are more motivated to read and have higher reading achievement scores than do students who lack such interactions (Campbell, Hombo, & Mazzeo, 2000). Students benefit from opportunities to talk about books with their peers and often motivate one another to read interesting books by sharing.

One example of a way to share is Quick Share, a simple strategy that takes only a few minutes to employ. Following independent reading time, the teacher asks students to find a partner. Each student has one minute to share information about the book he or she read during independent reading time. Another strategy is to place all the students' names in a fishbowl. Each day, after independent reading time is concluded, the teacher draws two or three names from the fishbowl. These children are then given an opportunity to share with the class what they have been reading.

These five questions posed are designed to guide administrators in assessing the classroom cultures within their schools and suggest ways they may promote motivation for reading. They address the essentials of classrooms that reflect a high value of reading and encourage the students' expectancy of becoming independent, proficient readers. Answers to these five questions can be used to direct principals and other administrators in making recommendations regarding resources or methods based on best practices for encouraging motivating reading environments for students, as detailed in each of the five sections.

Conclusion

Educational leaders can make a positive difference in the literacy of young children when they encourage school and classroom environments that provide access to a wide range of texts, opportunities for students to choose their own reading materials, opportunities for students to learn to select appropriate-level texts, time for independent reading, and opportunities to talk about books.

All students deserve high-quality reading instruction in the areas of phonemic awareness, phonics, vocabulary, fluency, and comprehension as the Reading First initiative recommends. It is equally important that schools provide students with instruction that is grounded in research and intended to develop in students a clear "need to read." Most educators would agree that a central goal of reading instruction is to foster a lifelong love of reading, and an awareness of motivational research can guide us in creating classroom cultures that foster engaged and strategic readers.

REFERENCES

Allington, R.L. (1991). The legacy of "slow it down and make it more concrete." In J. Zutell & S. McCormick (Eds.), *Learner factors/teacher factors: Issues in literacy research and instruction* (40th yearbook of the National Reading Conference, pp. 19–30). Chicago: National Reading Conference.

Allington, R.L., & McGill-Franzen, A. (1993, October 13). What are they to read? Not all children, Mr. Riley, have easy access to books. *Education Week*, p. 26.

Allington, R.L., & McGill-Franzen, A. (2003). The impact of summer loss on the reading achievement gap. *Phi Delta Kappan, 85*(6), 68–75.

Almasi, J. (1995). The nature of fourth graders sociocognitive conflicts in peer-led and teacher-led discussions of literature. *Reading Research Quarterly, 30*(3), 314–351.

Anderman, E.M., & Midgley, C. (1992, August). *Student self-efficacy as a function of classroom goal orientation.* Paper presented at American Psychological Association, Washington, DC. (ERIC Document Reproduction Service No. 375 367)

Artley, S.A. (1975). Good teachers of reading: Who are they? *The Reading Teacher, 29*(1), 26–31.

Bandura, A., Barbaranelli, C., Caprara, G., & Pastorelli, C. (1996). Multifaceted impact of self-efficacy beliefs on academic functioning. *Child Development, 67*(3), 1206–1222.

Brophy, J. (2004). *Motivating students to learn* (2nd ed.). Mahwah, NJ: Erlbaum.

Cambourne, B. (1995). Toward an educationally relevant theory of literacy learning: Twenty years of inquiry. *The Reading Teacher, 49*(3), 182–190.

Campbell, J.R., Hombo, C.M., & Mazzeo, J. (2000). NAEP 1999 trends in academic progress: Three decades of student performance. *Education Statistics Quarterly, 2*(4), 31–36.

Cunningham, A.E., & Stanovich, K.E. (1998). What reading does for the mind. *American Educator, 22*(1–2), 8–15.

Cunningham, P.M., & Allington, R.L. (1999). *Classrooms that work: They can all read and write* (2nd ed.). New York: Addison-Wesley.

Gambrell, L.B. (1986). Reading in the primary grades: How often, how long? In M.R. Sampson (Ed.), *The pursuit of literacy: Early reading and writing* (pp. 102–107). Dubuque, IA: Kendall/Hunt.

Gambrell, L.B. (1993). *The impact of RUNNING START on the reading motivation and behavior of first-grade children* (Research Rep.). College Park: University of Maryland.

Gambrell, L.B. (1996). Creating classroom cultures that foster reading motivation. *The Reading Teacher, 50*(1), 14–25.

Gambrell, L.B., Wilson, R.M., & Gantt, W. (1981). Classroom observations of task-attending behaviors of good and poor readers. *Journal of Educational Research, 74*(6), 400–404.

Guthrie, J.T., & Wigfield, A. (1997). Reading engagement: A rationale for theory and teaching. In J.T. Guthrie & A. Wigfield (Eds.), *Reading engagement: Motivating readers through integrated instruction* (pp. 1–12). Newark, DE: International Reading Association.

Hayes, D.P., & Ahrens, M.G. (1988). Vocabulary simplification or children: A special case of "motherese"? *Journal of Child Language, 15*(2), 395–410.

International Reading Association. (2000). *Providing books and other print materials for classroom and school libraries* (Position statement). Newark, DE: Author.

Maehr, M.L. (1984). Meaning and motivation: Toward a theory of personal investment. In R.E. Ames & C. Ames (Eds.), *Research on motivation in education: Student motivation* (Vol. 1, pp. 115–144). Orlando, FL: Academic Press.

McCombs, B.I. (1989). Self-regulated learning and academic achievement: A phenomenological view. In B.J. Zimmerman & D.H. Schunk (Eds.), *Self-regulated learning and achievement: Theory, research, and practice* (pp. 51–82). New York: Springer-Verlag.

Morrow, L.M. (1992). The impact of a literature-based program on literacy achievement, use of literature, and attitudes of children from minority backgrounds. *Reading Research Quarterly, 27*(3), 250–275.

Nagy, W.E., & Anderson, R.C. (1984). How many words are there in printed school English? *Reading Research Quarterly, 19*(3), 304–330.

National Institute of Child Health and Human Development. (2000). *Report of the National Reading Panel. Teaching children to read: An evidence-based assessment of the scientific research literature on reading and its implications for reading instruction* (NIH Publication No. 00-4769). Washington, DC: U.S. Government Printing Office.

Neuman, S.B., & Celano, D. (2001). Access to print in low-income and middle-income communities: An ecological study in four neighborhoods. *Reading Research Quarterly, 36*(1), 8–26.

No Child Left Behind Act of 2001, Pub. L. No. 107-110, 115 Stat. 1425 (2002). Retrieved October 1, 2005, from http://edworkforce.house.gov/issues/107th/education/nclb/nclb.htm

Oldfather, P. (1993). What students say about motivating experiences in a whole language classroom. *The Reading Teacher, 46*(8), 672–681.

Palmer, B.M., Codling, R.M., & Gambrell, L.B. (1994). In their own words: What elementary students have to say about motivation to read. *The Reading Teacher, 48*(2), 176–179.

Pekrun, R. (1993). Facets of adolescents' academic motivation: A longitudinal expectancy–value approach. In P.R. Pintrich & M.L. Maehr (Eds.), *New directions in measures and methods: Advances in motivation and achievement* (pp. 139–189). Greenwich, CT: JAI.

Reutzel, D.R., & Cooter, R.B. (2004). *Teaching children to read: Putting the pieces together* (4th ed.). Upper Saddle River, NJ: Merrill Prentice Hall.

Schiefele, U. (1991). Interest, learning, and motivation. *Educational Psychologist, 26*(3), 299–323.

Schunk, D.H. (1998). Goal and self-evaluative influences during children's cognitive skill learning. *American Educational Research Journal, 33*(3), 359–382.

Schunk, D.H., & Zimmerman, B.J. (1997). Social origins of self-regulating competence. *Educational Psychologist, 32*(4), 195–205.

Spaulding, C.L. (1992). The motivation to read and write. In J.W. Irwin & M.A. Doyle (Eds.), *Reading/writing connections: Learning from research* (pp. 177–201). Newark, DE: International Reading Association.

Stanovich, K.E. (1986). Matthew effects in reading: Some consequences of individual differences in the acquisition of literacy. *Reading Research Quarterly, 21*(4), 360–407.

Taylor, B.M., Frye, B.J., & Maruyama, G.M. (1990). Time spent reading and reading growth. *American Educational Research Journal, 27*(2), 351–362.

Wigfield, A., & Eccles, J. (2000). Expectancy–value theory of achievement motivation. *Contemporary Educational Psychology, 25*(1), 68–81.

CHAPTER 10

Critical Factors in Designing an Effective Reading Intervention for Struggling Readers

Richard L. Allington

JEROME, a fourth-grade struggling reader, can read books from the Junie B. Jones and Polk Street School series with reasonable accuracy, but he reads slowly and without much fluency. He has struggled with reading and writing since kindergarten—at least in comparison to most of his peers. He is a bright and easygoing child, an accomplished athlete for his age, and well liked by his classmates and adored by his teachers. He's not a nonreader, but he has little opportunity to demonstrate fluent reading in his classroom, where he experiences whole-class reading lessons drawn from the grade-level commercial reading series that was marketed as a "scientific" solution. Unfortunately for Jerome, and other struggling readers, grade-level reading series offer teachers little in the way of support for struggling readers (McGill-Franzen, Solic, Zmach, & Zeig, in press).

Jerome also participates in a 30-minute small-group remedial reading intervention two times a week. Jerome attends with five of his classmates, who also are struggling with reading, although for different reasons. The intervention removes them from a segment of the whole-class reading lesson every Monday and Wednesday and focuses primarily on working with a paraprofessional to

Understanding and Implementing Reading First Initiatives: The Changing Role of Administrators by Carrice Cummins, Editor. Copyright © 2006 by the International Reading Association.

complete various skills using worksheets from a supplemental reading program used in the intervention classes.

Jerome and his peers read aloud the worksheets with the paraprofessional, who provides corrections to words they cannot pronounce. Students then attempt to figure out what response they are to provide. When they encounter difficulties, the paraprofessional will often read aloud the supplemental worksheets. She then checks to make sure each student has correctly completed the worksheet item. If the worksheet tasks are completed before the intervention period is over, Jerome and his peers are allowed to play one of several computer-based games, often focused on decoding words but not words from either classroom or intervention reading materials. When they return to the classroom, they hand in their worksheets and take up whatever work their classmates are doing.

The No Child Left Behind Act of 2001 (2002) requires that reading instruction provided to students be based in "scientific research." Although there has been much concern about the federal definition of what constitutes "scientific research" in reading (Allington, 2004; Coles, 2001; Cunningham, 2001; Garan, 2001), it does not seem unreasonable to expect that research would inform the design of interventions for struggling readers (Allington, 2002, 2006). One problem may be that too often the research focus in designing reading instruction is on the relatively narrow band of topics that the National Reading Panel (NRP) reviewed in 2000. Another problem is that some of those findings have been distorted in the advice provided to those designing reading interventions.

For instance, the widely distributed document *Put Reading First: The Research Building Blocks for Reading Success* (National Institute for Literacy [NIFL], 2001) suggests that "systematic and explicit phonics instruction is particularly beneficial for children who are having difficulty learning to read...and in helping children overcome reading difficulties" (p. 15). However, the report of the NRP (National Institute of Child Health and Human Development, 2000) actually concluded that, "Phonics instruction failed to exert a significant impact on the reading performance of low-achieving readers in 2nd through 6th grade" (p. 2-133).

Put Reading First contains a number of other misrepresentations, including suggestions that decodable text has been shown to be a necessary component of "scientific" reading instruction and that "add-on" phonics programs are ineffective. Timothy Shanahan (2003), a member of the NRP, has commented on this last suggestion that "NRP did not find that and, given the nature of the research findings we reported on phonics, I would be surprised if the statement were true" (p. 647).

But debating the merits of decodable texts, add-on phonics programs, or any sort of phonics program in the design of effective reading interventions for struggling readers may be beside the point. Situations might exist where one might elect to use decodable texts for some poor readers, for example, or an add-on phonics program such as Cunningham's (2004) interactive Word Maker software. In discussing the design of effective interventions, we may lose sight of the forest while debating the advantages of particular types of trees. That is, we need to worry about broad research-based design principles first, then worry about the details of the instruction because those details will vary, one hopes, for every struggling reader. The example of Jerome at the beginning of this chapter helps illustrate how the best intended intervention designs are often markedly problematic given what we know about effective intervention design. Thus, this chapter presents four research-based design principles. School administrators should monitor interventions for struggling readers to ensure that each of these principles is reflected in the daily reading instruction provided to struggling readers. (See Table 10.1 for an example of a simple, effective monitoring strategy.)

• Table 10.1 •
Monitoring Strategy

Randomly select five struggling readers, perhaps one from each grade level. Visit the classrooms these students are assigned to and spend 10–20 minutes simply observing the struggling reader and the lesson being offered. Ask the student about the reading he or she does in school each day. Ask the student if he or she reads more than other students in the class on a regular basis. You may want to ask the student to read a bit in a soft voice from the curriculum materials in use. Ask yourself, Can the student read this accurately, fluently, and with comprehension? In regard to the lesson, Do you see good examples of explicit and useful strategy teaching? Later in the day, meet with the student's intervention teacher and ask him or her to tell you about the classroom program you observed. Ask for a description of what the student did during the intervention class. Then, determine whether or not the classroom and intervention lessons created a coherent and balanced reading program.

Four Research-Based Design Principles for Helping Struggling Readers

Reading Volume

If we intend to accelerate the reading development of struggling readers, intend to help them "catch up" with their classmates who are developing typically as readers and writers, then we will necessarily have to ensure that the intervention design provides expanded opportunities to engage in successful reading practice. One of the misunderstandings of the findings of the NRP is linked to this issue. Some educators suggest the NRP report recommended that, "rather than allocating instructional time for independent reading in the classroom, encourage your students to read more outside of school" (NIFL, 2001, p. 29). But that is not quite what the NRP said. As panelist Shanahan (2003) writes, "In fact, the panel did not conclude that children did not need reading practice, only that how this might be best accomplished is an open question" (p. 653). The NRP found that none of the popular methods or packages (e.g., Sustained Silent Reading [SSR], Drop Everything and Read [DEAR], Book It, or Accelerated Reader) that are intended to increase reading volume had much evidence suggesting that once implemented, reading volume actually increased.

Nonetheless, reading volume is important. Reading is like virtually every human proficiency in that practice matters. Practice alone is not sufficient to develop proficiency; however, instruction is also required. But practice—reading volume—is an important factor in the design of reading interventions. Guthrie (2004) has pointed out that the best readers spend about 500% more time engaged in reading than do the least proficient readers. He suggests that the relation between reading volume and reading proficiency is not coincidental. Drawing on research from a wide array of human activity (sports, chess, music, and so forth), he reports that the highly skilled individuals routinely engage in far more practice than those who are less skilled. His conclusion: "Because engaged readers spend 500% more time reading than disengaged students, educators should attempt to increase engaged reading time by 200%–500%" (p. 1).

Let's consider Jerome, the student mentioned at the beginning of the chapter. At best, his instruction provides him the opportunity to read a single story or story excerpt each week, given his participation in the whole-class reading series lesson. Under the best of circumstances, Jerome will read no more than the better readers in his classroom.

Because the grade-level text is difficult for him, he may actually read less. But even if he reads the 20 minutes per day that typical fourth graders do during their reading lessons, Guthrie argues for the need to increase his volume to around 100 minutes per day. That is not occurring now for Jerome.

Depending on the scheduling of his intervention, Jerome even misses some classroom reading opportunities while completing the worksheets. Nothing in the design of the classroom instruction or the intervention ensures that Jerome will have greater opportunities to practice reading than his more skilled classmates. The other design problem is that Jerome's reading is almost always from grade-level texts, even though Jerome is at least a year below grade level in his reading development.

Jerome needs an intervention design that will dramatically increase his reading volume. This could be done by having his classroom provide Jerome and his struggling peers with a second daily reading lesson, an intervention documented as effective (Taylor, Short, Shearer, & Frye, 1995). But adding a second 30-minute guided reading group would still be far shy of the 100 minutes of reading practice. If we added 40 minutes of reading practice in a daily after-school program, we could reach the 100 minutes. Or we could ensure he has 40 minutes of independent reading time every day. The point is that reading volume has been widely neglected in the design of interventions for struggling readers. This may be one reason why most struggling readers continue to struggle year after year.

Appropriate Texts

If we intend to increase the reading volume of struggling readers, we must be concerned about the books provided for them to read. In the first recent experimental test comparing the outcomes for struggling readers tutored using grade-level materials (texts used in the classroom) or reading-level materials (texts matched to reading level of students), O'Connor and her colleagues (2002) found a clear advantage for using texts matched to struggling readers' reading levels. This was especially true for those students with the lowest levels of proficiency, where significant greater gains were found on decoding, word identification, and fluency.

But there has been evidence of the importance of matching readers with books they can read accurately, fluently, and with good comprehension since Betts's (1949) classic study. In fact, designing interventions for struggling readers has always had the use of appropriate difficulty texts as a standard. Nonetheless, it is incredibly common to observe struggling readers assigned grade-level texts not just for their classroom reading lessons, but also to have those same too difficult texts used in their intervention lessons in the reading or resource room or the after-school program.

Struggling readers need books they can read accurately, fluently, and with strong comprehension all day long. We cannot expect to accelerate the reading development of struggling readers by providing appropriately difficult books just during the intervention session. Thirty minutes of instruction and practice in an appropriate text during a daily intervention session will not overcome 300 minutes of time in texts that are too difficult during the remainder of the day. It is not just during the classroom reading lesson and the intervention lesson that struggling readers need books they can read successfully. Struggling readers also need texts of appropriate difficulty during science and social studies. And they need appropriate books to read at home in the evening, on weekends, and over the summer months (Allington & McGill-Franzen, 2003).

Based on the research available, I suggest that struggling readers should spend about 80% of their school reading time in texts they read with 99% accuracy, fluently in phrases with intonation, and with 90% comprehension or better. This is just the sort of reading diet we routinely provide our best readers, those reading above grade level. Every year our best readers expand the gap between their reading proficiency and the reading proficiency of their struggling reader classmates. Yet, in too many schools, the struggling readers are struggling in the same reading series, the same social studies texts, and the same class novels that their better reading peers read accurately, fluently, and with good comprehension.

High-success reading produces higher levels of self-efficacy and motivation to read. The only way we might meet Guthrie's target of dramatically expanding the reading volume of struggling readers is to ensure that their desks are filled with books they can read easily and successfully, all day long.

Explicit and Personalized Instruction

Struggling readers need personalized and explicit instruction. Practice alone is not sufficient. Returning to Jerome, his reading lessons provide some whole-class instruction, but too often the lessons found in commercial reading series provide little or no explicit instruction (McGill-Franzen et al., in press). The most common lessons are often actually assessments. Lessons where comprehension questions, for instance, are viewed as the comprehension instructional component. Or decoding lessons where fill-in-the-missing-vowel worksheets are viewed as phonics lessons. But students who can answer the questions do not benefit from answering, at least in terms of extending their comprehension strategies. And students who cannot answer do not learn what strategy, or strategies, they needed to employ to derive the answer. Students who can fill in the correct vowel learn nothing from the worksheet and neither do the students who fill in the wrong vowels.

Such common activities, questions after reading and worksheets of various sorts, may be useful if the teacher uses them to identify students who need explicit instruction, that is, if after noting which students were unsuccessful, the teacher pulls those students together for an appropriate strategy lesson. But if the postreading questions and worksheets produce no reteaching, then the time spent on those activities is largely wasted because neither the better nor the struggling readers benefit in any way from completing the activity.

In the other chapters of this book, you will find any number of suggestions for useful and explicit strategy teaching. In addition, there are a number of other resources that will prove useful: *Explaining Reading: A Research for Teaching Concepts, Skills, and Strategies* (Duffy, 2003); *Teaching Strategic Processes in Reading* (Almasi, 2003); *Improving Comprehension With Think-Aloud Strategies* (Wilhelm, 2001); and *Strategies That Work: Teaching Comprehension to Enhance Understanding* (Harvey & Goudvis, 2000). Each of these texts, and many others, provides superb guidance for learning how to teach reading explicitly and strategically. Every school should consider using any of these titles for teachers as professional readers (TAPR) study groups. TAPR groups involve selecting professional texts that will be read and discussed with teaching peers (Allington & Cunningham, 2002). This form of professional development is essential if teachers are to build expertise across their career spans. It is essential if students like Jerome are to ever end their struggles.

Another design feature that must be considered is that of providing more intensive personalized teaching for students who struggle. The research available demonstrates that one-to-one expert tutoring is simply the most powerful intervention model. Camilli, Vargas, and Yurecko (2003) reanalyzed the NRP data and found that tutoring had an effect size that was twice as large as that reported for systematic phonics instruction. Likewise, a recent meta-analysis (D'Agostino & Murphy, 2004) of 36 studies of the effectiveness of Reading Recovery, probably the most widely implemented tutoring intervention, found that intervention produced significant growth in reading as measured on both instructionally sensitive and standardized reading achievement tests. These reports echo earlier large-scale analyses that found tutoring to be the most effective intervention design (Shanahan, 1998; Wasik & Slavin, 1993), especially expert tutoring.

But while the research often cited as supporting the goal of all children reading on level by third grade invariably used tutoring interventions, the costs of providing tutoring to struggling readers is enormous; neither state nor federal education funding streams provide the monies needed to implement tutoring on a broad scale (Allington, 2004). Nonetheless, tutoring must be considered for those students who have fallen the furthest behind.

There is evidence, though, that suggests that very small group interventions (two to three students) can be quite effective (Allington, 2002; Mathes et al., 2005; Pinnell, Lyons, Deford, Bryk, & Seltzer, 1994; Vaughn, Gersten, & Chard, 2000). Very small group interventions seem to work well when members of the group share instructional needs. Grouping children by instructional levels and instructional needs would make it more likely that all members of the group will benefit from a single lesson. There is little evidence, unfortunately, that intervention groups like Jerome's, six students with varying instructional needs, can provide the support needed to accelerate reading development. Worse in Jerome's case is the reliance on paraprofessional staff to deliver the intervention. What Jerome needs is the most expert instruction available, not the least expert.

Although there have been occasional accounts of training programs for paraprofessionals that produced interventions that resulted in modest reading growth, the larger research base suggests little or no benefit for paraprofessional-based interventions (Boyd-Zaharias & Pate-Bain, 1998; Rowan & Guthrie, 1989; Rubin & Long, 1994). In other words, the research indicates struggling readers need expert teachers providing the intervention, not paraprofessionals or willing but untrained volunteers.

Coherence and Balance

Finally, intervention design must work to ensure both coherence and balance. In a study that interviewed both classroom and intervention teachers (remedial reading, Title I, and resource room teachers), almost no classroom teachers could reliably discuss what students from their classrooms did during intervention lessons (Johnston, Allington, & Afflerbach, 1985). Likewise, very few intervention teachers could even name the reading curriculum materials that their intervention students used during classroom reading lessons. In over half the cases, the two teachers (classroom and intervention) were using reading curriculum materials that were strategically incompatible—materials more likely to confuse the struggling reader than help him (McGill-Franzen & Allington, 1990). The lack of shared knowledge about the reading lessons offered produced a fragmented and incoherent instructional experience, rather than a consistent and balanced curriculum plan. Struggling readers seem to benefit more from coherent and supportive interventions than from interventions like Jerome's that have them struggling in two different reading programs.

One caution is needed, however. Some classroom reading plans are unbalanced. Some plans overemphasize certain critical elements of reading while largely ignoring others. For instance, a classroom plan might overemphasize oral reading, or maybe oral reading rate, while neglecting silent reading and reading comprehension. A coherent and balanced plan would not simply replicate the imbalance of the classroom in the intervention lesson (Johnston & Allington, 1991). Rather, the focus during intervention might shift to silent reading and comprehension. However, if the classroom reading materials are inappropriate, say, too difficult, then replacing those materials while focusing on silent reading and comprehension would provide the balance needed.

But in designing effective reading instruction for struggling readers, educators simply cannot allow students to continue using inappropriate materials in the classroom. Remember the previously stated goal: Students should have high-quality reading instruction all day long. Thus, the classroom teacher might use the same materials used by the intervention teacher and perhaps continue the focus on oral reading. The intervention teacher then reuses those materials in lessons but provides both targeted strategy instruction and a silent reading and comprehension focus.

The basic design features here are simple: coherence and balance. For too long remedial and special education interventions have been unhinged from the core curriculum. The result is that the most fragile learners have been provided an often dizzying array of materials and lessons—an incoherent array that is not experienced by students developing their reading with little difficulty.

Conclusion

Educators can design research-based interventions that will accelerate the reading development of struggling readers. But the four design features presented in this chapter are critically important for struggling readers.

The intervention plan must

- substantially expand the volume of daily reading;
- ensure access to appropriate texts all day long;
- provide needed expert, explicit, personalized instruction; and
- craft a coherent and balanced array of reading lessons and activities.

Effective intervention designs cannot be achieved simply by purchasing an alternative curriculum package that will be delivered to the struggling readers with little regard to individual needs or the whole-day instructional experience (Allington & Nowak, 2004). Effective interventions cannot be designed in isolation from the whole-day instructional experiences of struggling readers. Enhancing classroom reading lessons first and then focusing on providing more intensive, more personalized, and more expert reading instruction to students who still struggle is the only solution.

REFERENCES

Allington, R.L. (2002). Research on reading/learning disability interventions. In A.E. Farstrup & S.J. Samuels (Eds.), *What research says about reading instruction* (3rd ed., pp. 261–290). Newark, DE: International Reading Association.

Allington, R.L. (2004). Setting the record straight. *Educational Leadership, 61*(6), 22–25.

Allington, R.L. (2006). *What really matters for struggling readers: Designing research-based programs* (2nd ed.). Boston: Allyn & Bacon.

Allington, R.L., & Cunningham, P.M. (2002). *Schools that work: Where all children read and write* (2nd ed.). Boston: Allyn & Bacon.

Allington, R.L., & McGill-Franzen, A.M. (2003). The impact of summer loss on the reading achievement gap. *Phi Delta Kappan, 85*(1), 68–75.

Allington, R.L., & Nowak, R. (2004). "Proven programs" and other unscientific ideas. In C.C. Block, D. Lapp, E.J. Cooper, J. Flood, N. Roser, & J.V. Tinajero (Eds.), *Teaching all the children: Strategies for developing literacy in an urban setting* (pp. 93–102). New York: Guilford.

Almasi, J.F. (2003). *Teaching strategic processes in reading.* New York: Guilford.

Betts, E.A. (1949). Adjusting instruction to individual needs. In N.B. Henry (Ed.), *The forty-eighth yearbook of the National Society for the Study of Education: Part II, Reading in the elementary school* (pp. 266–283). Chicago: University of Chicago.

Boyd-Zaharias, J., & Pate-Bain, H. (1998). *Teacher aides and student learning: Lessons from Project STAR.* Arlington, VA: Educational Research Service.

Camilli, G., Vargas, S., & Yurecko, M. (2003). "Teaching children to read": The fragile link between science and federal education policy. *Education Policy Analysis Archives, 11*(15). Retrieved May 20, 2003, from http://epaa.asu.edu/epaa/v11/n15

Coles, G. (2001). Reading taught to the tune of the "scientific" hickory stick. *Phi Delta Kappan, 83*(3), 205–212.

Cunningham, J.W. (2001). Essay book review: The National Reading Panel report. *Reading Research Quarterly, 36*(3), 326–335.

Cunningham, P. (2004). *Word maker* [computer software]. Volo, IL: Don Johnston, Inc.

D'Agostino, J.V., & Murphy, J.A. (2004). A meta-analysis of Reading Recovery in United States schools. *Educational Evaluation and Policy Analysis, 26*(1), 23–38.

Duffy, G.G. (2003). *Explaining reading: A resource for teaching concepts, skills, and strategies.* New York: Guilford.

Garan, E.M. (2001). Beyond the smoke and mirrors: A critique of the National Reading Panel Report on phonics. *Phi Delta Kappan, 82*(7), 500–506.

Guthrie, J.T. (2004). Teaching for literacy engagement. *Journal of Literacy Research, 36*(1), 1–28.

Harvey, S., & Goudvis, A. (2000). *Strategies that work: Teaching comprehension to enhance understanding.* York, ME: Stenhouse.

Johnston, P.A., & Allington, R.L. (1991). Remediation. In R. Barr, M.L. Kamil, P. Mosenthal, & P.D. Pearson (Eds.), *Handbook of reading research* (Vol. 2, pp. 984–1012). New York: Longman.

Johnston, P., Allington, R.L., & Afflerbach, P. (1985). The congruence of classroom and remedial reading instruction. *The Elementary School Journal, 85*(4), 465–478.

Mathes, P.G., Denton, C.A., Fletcher, J.M., Anthony, J.L., Francis, D.J., & Schatschneider, C. (2005). The effects of theoretically different instruction and student characteristics on the skills of struggling readers. *Reading Research Quarterly, 40*(2), 148–182.

McGill-Franzen, A., & Allington, R.L. (1990). Comprehension and coherence: Neglected elements of literacy instruction in remedial and resource room services. *Journal of Reading, Writing, and Learning Disabilities, 6*(2), 149–182.

McGill-Franzen, A., Solic, K.J., Zmach, C., & Zeig, J.L. (in press). The confluence of two policy mandates: Core reading programs and 3rd grade retention. *The Elementary School Journal.*

National Institute of Child Health and Human Development. (2000). *Report of the National Reading Panel. Teaching children to read: An evidence-based assessment of the scientific research literature on reading and its implications for reading instruction* (NIH Publication No. 00-4769). Washington, DC: U.S. Government Printing Office.

National Institute for Literacy (NIFL). (2001). *Put reading first: The research building blocks for reading success.* Washington, DC: Author

No Child Left Behind Act of 2001, Pub. L. No. 107-110, 115 Stat. 1425 (2002). Retrieved October 1, 2005, from http://edworkforce.house.gov/issues/107th/education/nclb/nclb.htm

O'Connor, R.E., Bell, K.M., Harty, K.R., Larkin, L.K., Sackor, S.M., & Zigmond, N. (2002). Teaching reading to poor readers in the intermediate grades: A comparison of text difficulty. *Journal of Educational Psychology, 94*(3), 474–485.

Pinnell, G.S., Lyons, C.A., Deford, D.E., Bryk, A.S., & Seltzer, M. (1994). Comparing instructional models for the literacy education of high-risk first graders. *Reading Research Quarterly, 29*(1), 8–39.

Rowan, B., & Guthrie, L.F. (1989). The quality of Chapter 1 instruction: Results from a study of twenty-four schools. In R.E. Slavin, N. Karweit, & N. Madden (Eds.), *Effective programs for students at risk* (pp. 195–219). Boston: Allyn & Bacon.

Rubin, P.M., & Long, R.M. (1994). Who is teaching our children? Implications of the use of aides in Chapter 1. *ERS Spectrum, 12*(2), 28–34.

Shanahan, T. (1998). On the effectiveness and limitations of tutoring. In P.D. Pearson & P.A. Iran-Nejad (Ed.), *Review of research in education* (Vol. 23, pp. 217–234). Washington, DC: American Educational Research Association.

Shanahan, T. (2003). Research-based reading instruction: Myths about the National Reading Panel report. *The Reading Teacher, 56*(7), 646–655.

Taylor, B., Short, R., Shearer, B., & Frye, B. (1995). First grade teachers provide early reading intervention in the classroom. In R.L. Allington & S.A. Walmsley, *No quick fix: Rethinking literacy programs in America's elementary schools* (pp. 159–178). Newark, DE: International Reading Association; New York: Teachers College Press.

Vaughn, S., Gersten, R., & Chard, D.J. (2000). The underlying message in LD intervention research: Findings from research syntheses. *Exceptional Children, 67*(1), 99–114.

Wasik, B.A., & Slavin, R.E. (1993). Preventing early reading failure with one-to-one tutoring: A review of five programs. *Reading Research Quarterly, 28*(2), 178–200.

Wilhelm, J.D. (2001). *Improving comprehension with think-aloud strategies*. New York: Scholastic.

CHAPTER 11

The Literacy Coach as a Catalyst for Change

Rita M. Bean and Kathryn E. Carroll

MS. RUSSELL, an elementary school principal, and Ms. Franklin, literacy coach at the school, begin their weekly meeting. The focus of this meeting is to review the scores on the screening tests given to second graders. They begin by reviewing the test results (on fluency, sight word, and decoding) given to the second graders. As they go through the data, they look for patterns in the scores. This helps them begin to think about the instruction that needs to take place in classrooms.

They notice that in each classroom there are several students who score below "benchmark" on each of the measures. They discuss several ideas about how they might help teachers think about planning for these struggling readers, such as modifying instruction, incorporating some flexible grouping, involving the reading specialist, providing additional resources, and so forth. To end their meeting, they discuss their responsibilities as principal and as literacy coach in getting this information to teachers and being certain that the necessary strategies are carried out with students. They leave the meeting with a better understanding of what the strengths and areas of need are for the second graders and what each of them has to do to work with teachers in improving reading instruction.

Understanding and Implementing Reading First Initiatives: The Changing Role of Administrators by Carrice Cummins, Editor. Copyright © 2006 by the International Reading Association.

The meeting of a principal and a literacy coach, previously described, provides an example of how these two professionals in leadership roles can work together to plan professional development for teachers that will have an impact on classroom practices, and ultimately, student achievement. The emphasis on professional development in Reading First, a part of the No Child Left Behind Act of 2001 (2002), is an indication of the importance of teachers and the instruction they provide. Likewise, the emphasis on literacy coaches in schools in Reading First legislation helps recognize the need for school leaders to rethink the ways in which professional development is provided.

Not all professional development is created equal. In *What Matters Most: Teaching for America's Future* (1996), the National Commission on Teaching and America's Future calls for professional development that is long term and systematic. Professional development, to facilitate actual change in instructional practice, should also provide opportunities for teachers to learn new information and to receive support and feedback as they are applying what they are learning (Cooter, 2003; Darling-Hammond & McLaughlin, 1995; Joyce & Showers, 1995, 2002). Joyce and Showers (1995), for example, discuss the importance of knowing exactly what outcomes one hopes that professional development programs will achieve. They identify the following potential outcomes: development of new knowledge or understandings; changes in attitude toward children or instruction; and development of specific instructional skills, or the consistent and appropriate use of new skills and strategies in the classroom—that is, the transfer of new learning to classroom practice. In their studies, Joyce and Showers (2002) also indicate that professional development programs that included in-class coaching were more successful in increasing such transfer. Indeed, they indicate that such in-class coaching produced "a large and dramatic increase in transfer" (p. 77).

Evidence such as this has generated support for literacy coaches in schools. For the purposes of this chapter, we define literacy coaches as master teachers who have the ability to work effectively with other teachers to lead and enhance the literacy instruction provided in schools. Thus, to use literacy coaches as a resource in the school, administrators need to (1) establish a list of duties that literacy coaches might fulfill, (2) identify characteristics and criteria to use in selecting literacy coaches, and (3) develop an understanding of how they might facilitate the role of the coach (e.g., having an awareness of guidelines or suggestions that will enable coaches to be more effective in their work).

Duties of Literacy Coaches

Literacy coaches can work with teachers in a number of ways to facilitate change, from providing appropriate materials and resources to observing teachers and providing feedback about instruction. In other words, there is a continuum of activities that literacy coaches can undertake. Decisions about how to work with specific teachers must be made based on the readiness of each teacher to work with the coach, the experiences and knowledge of the coach, and the context of the situation. Literacy coaches may first want to work with teachers in ways that are low risk—that is, there will be little chance that the teacher will view the literacy coach's involvement as one of evaluation. Activities such as assisting with assessment (as a means of helping the teacher and modeling appropriate instructional strategies), building content knowledge (by leading a workshop for a group of teachers), or providing resources for teachers who have specific needs (books that students can read to practice fluency) are nonthreatening activities that can improve classroom practices and at the same time provide for the development of a trusting relationship between the literacy coach and teachers. Table 11.1 provides a sampling of activities that literacy coaches can undertake in their role.

Although it is essential that literacy coaches take into consideration the readiness of the teacher in working with them, the knowledge and experience of coaches also plays an important role in how they view and carry out their jobs. For example, coaches may feel quite comfortable assessing students in the classroom and even modeling specific strategies such as building phonemic awareness through segmenting and blending activities or teaching high-level decoding skills. Some coaches also may be able to lead small-discussion groups (e.g., grade level, curriculum, or study groups). Others, however, may have little experience with or knowledge about making presentations to large groups of teachers in an effective manner. They also may lack information about how and what to observe, or how to provide feedback to teachers about what is going on in their classrooms and the steps that can be taken to improve instruction for students. In other words, some literacy coaches may have in-depth content knowledge about literacy but may not be as knowledgeable about their roles as change agents. Coaches can begin their work where they feel comfortable but cannot lose sight of the fact that, to be successful at coaching, they must work toward becoming proficient in areas beyond their comfort zone.

Finally, literacy coaches must have a good understanding of the context in which they work. Even if everything else is in place for

• Table 11.1 •
Activities of Literacy Coaches

Activity	Description
Holding meetings	Leading or participating in meetings (e.g., grade-level meetings, curriculum meetings). Example: Coach meets with grade-level teachers to discuss assessment data and how the results should be used to modify instruction.
Planning and organizing	Preparing for a model lesson, coteaching, and so forth, or organizing and obtaining materials for a specific teacher or teachers. Example: Coach is going to conduct a model lesson on phonemic awareness and wants to develop manipulative materials for the students.
Assessing students	Assessing students as a means of helping the classroom teacher gain a better understanding of students' strengths and needs. Example: Coach, together with the classroom teacher, does the progress-monitoring testing of all students in grade 3.
Modeling and demonstrating	Demonstrating specific strategies or procedures to help teachers gain a better understanding of how to use them in the classroom. Example: Coach models a specific vocabulary building lesson for second-grade teachers.
Coteaching	Teaching a group or the class along with the classroom teacher. This activity is undertaken primarily to enhance teachers' knowledge of specific approaches or strategies but also can assist teachers in differentiating instruction for students. Example: Teacher and coach coteach a phonics lesson. One person is responsible for most of the whole-class instruction, and one person is responsible for monitoring students' work and recognizing students' efforts.
Instructing students	Teaching a group of students to provide the reading instruction that they need. This can occur in the classroom or on a pull-out basis. In this case, the focus is on providing appropriate instruction for students. Example: Coach pulls out third graders from several classrooms to provide supplemental fluency instruction.
Performing outreach work	Assisting in the work done with parents by meeting with them as a group (e.g., providing information about the reading program in the school, helping them understand how they can work effectively with their children). Coaches also work with other agencies (e.g., library, university) to promote special programs that enhance reading instruction.

(continued)

• Table 11.1 •
Activities of Literacy Coaches (continued)

Activity	Description
	Example: Coach works with a university to develop a program in which undergraduate students come to the school and work with struggling readers.
Attending professional development programs	Attending meetings to increase their knowledge and understanding of literacy instruction and assessment or how to coach effectively. Example: Coach attends meetings about how to use data for instructional decision making.
Visiting classrooms	Observing in the classroom as a means of learning more about how instruction is being provided. Generally, this includes three steps: (1) preconference with the teacher to set a goal for the observation, (2) the observation, and (3) a postconference in which the teacher and coach meet to discuss the observation. Example: Teacher asks coach to observe how she is conducting a discussion group. She asks the coach to consider the following: Is she involving all students? What is the nature of the questioning?
Conducting professional development sessions	Providing information to a group of teachers using a more traditional workshop format. Example: Coach attends a professional development seminar, Making the Most of Your Instructional Time, and prepares a similar presentation for all primary-grade teachers as a means of sharing the information.

changes to occur, if the culture of the school is overlooked, reform may not happen. The role of the administrator is crucial. Literacy coaches need the support and guidance of the principal, and other involved administrators, if they are to be effective. If principals see the coach only as someone who serves in an administrative or managerial function (e.g., ordering and distributing material) or as an individual whose major role is working with students, there is little chance that the coach will have the opportunity to facilitate change within a school. Administrators at both the school and district levels must be knowledgeable about the role of the literacy coach and be supportive of that role. Principals can help support the literacy coach by providing resources and a schedule that promote the work of the coaches. They can develop incentives to encourage teachers and staff to accept and even appreciate change. To do so, administrators need to consider the following three questions:

(1) What should the literacy coach be doing to improve classroom instruction? (2) What is my role in improving classroom instruction? and (3) How should we work together to improve instruction?

Scheduling is an important aspect to consider. Many literacy coaches with whom we have talked complain about the lack of time available to them to engage in what they consider to be the most meaningful aspects of their job. They are so busy organizing materials, assessing students, or analyzing assessment data that they have little time to interact with teachers. Or, even if they have the time, it is difficult to schedule meetings with teachers who may be reluctant to give up planning time or meet before or after school. Some literacy coaches have found it effective to work with one grade level at a time (e.g., they may focus on third-grade classes for a six-week period). They schedule grade-level meetings to discuss test data and the literacy goals for third grade. They meet individually with these teachers to look at the performance of students in specific classrooms. They model lessons in each of the classrooms, focusing on the needs and goals of the teachers. They also go through the coaching cycle with each of the teachers by first talking with them prior to observing them, then observing them, and finally talking with them about that observation. This approach, in addition to providing a workable schedule, can help the literacy coach become well acquainted with the curriculum and instruction of a specific grade level.

By reflecting on their roles in schools and seeking feedback and advice from teachers, principals and literacy coaches can gain a better sense of what is needed to improve reading instruction in their schools. Such reflection can occur in small-group meetings in a more structured format such as grade-level or curriculum group meetings or informally, with teachers, the literacy coach, and the principal talking together about school improvement. During these meetings, literacy coaches also can seek feedback from teachers that will help them think about how they perform their coaching duties.

Selecting Literacy Coaches

In reviewing job descriptions for literacy coaches, it is obvious that the literacy coach is expected to know and do a lot. For example, Figure 11.1 provides a sample job description for a literacy coach. Literacy coaches must have an in-depth understanding of literacy instruction and assessment, be effective teachers of literacy, be able to work well with adults in one-on-one and group situations, and be able to present information to other educators in an organized and succinct way. Adminis-

---

> ## • Figure 11.1 •
> ### Sample Job Description for Literacy Coach
>
> ---
>
> The literacy coach will...
>
> Assume leadership for the school reading program by developing plans with the principal for professional development of school personnel involved with teaching reading.
>
> Assume responsibility for providing professional development for school personnel (making presentations, forming study groups, and so forth) or for obtaining other appropriate professional development providers.
>
> Meet with teachers on a regular basis to establish goals for the literacy program and to develop instructional strategies and approaches to meet goals, which include determining curricular and instructional activities and grouping procedures necessary to meet the needs of each student.
>
> Implement an ongoing assessment program that includes screening, diagnostic, progress-monitoring, and outcome measures. This includes assisting teachers in administering instruments, interpreting the results, developing instruction that addresses students' needs, and maintaining accurate student records.
>
> Assist teachers in selecting appropriate supplementary and/or intervention materials for students who require additional instruction. This includes print and nonprint materials.
>
> Observe, furnish guided practice, and provide feedback to each classroom teacher on a regular basis during reading instruction time and/or during the reading enrichment period (for all K–3 teachers), focusing on the five essential elements of reading: phonemic awareness, phonics, fluency, vocabulary, and comprehension.
>
> Communicate effectively with parents regarding their children's progress in becoming efficient readers, and work with others to develop a parent involvement program for the school. Build relationships between preschools and after-school programs so there is appropriate transition and coordination between these programs and the school efforts.

---

trators should consider these categories essential as they select literacy coaches.

In fact, in the *Standards for Reading Professionals—Revised* (2003), the International Reading Association (IRA) suggests that literacy coaches need to meet the same criteria required of reading specialists. In other words, they should have a master's degree and classroom experience and be able to demonstrate the performance competencies identified in that document. The IRA position statement *The Role and Qualifications of the Reading Coach in the United States* (2004) also provides helpful information regarding literacy, or reading, coaches.

To begin, literacy coaches must have an in-depth knowledge base of literacy that enables them to interact comfortably with classroom teachers about research-based strategies, assessment and how to use it, and ways to modify instruction to meet the needs of students. They also should have knowledge about reading development so they can work with teachers at various grade levels.

Second, although in-depth content knowledge is important, literacy coaches also must have demonstrated that they are master teachers who have the respect of other teachers for their knowledge and teaching capabilities. Thus, literacy coaches should have experience with teaching diverse groups of students, especially those struggling to learn to read.

Third, literacy coaches must be able to work well with other adults. Without question, literacy coaches must have the interpersonal and communication skills that enable them to interact effectively with their peers. Teachers, like all adults faced with change, have different views about the change process and especially their involvement with a literacy coach. These views range from an excitement about this new possibility to acceptance to resistance. The literacy coach will have a difficult time making inroads if he or she does not have the preparation or experience related to fostering change in schools. Knowledge about adults and how they learn will enable literacy coaches to plan their work more effectively and also enable them to understand more fully why there may be differences in teachers' perceptions and responses to the suggested changes in teaching reading. The major responsibility of the literacy coach is the facilitation of adult learning; this shift from teaching children to teaching adults can be a difficult one for some coaches.

Finally, literacy coaches must be able to work effectively in a group setting, leading or participating in group discussion. They may need to work with grade-level or curriculum groups in ways that necessitate an ability to foster discussion and facilitate the work of the group. In addition, literacy coaches may be required to make presentations to an entire staff of teachers. In such cases, they need to have expertise in developing such presentations or workshops and an understanding of how to keep groups involved and motivated to learn.

Literacy coaches, therefore, must not only demonstrate effective teaching abilities but also have the leadership skills that enable them to become effective change agents in schools. Certainly, if a school district views a particular individual as having the potential to be a literacy coach, but the individual is lacking in certain experiences, the district can develop or provide various professional development opportunities for that individual. Such preparation is essential if the literacy coach is to succeed in his or her job. Attempting a role such as literacy coach can be discouraging if one does not have the skills or abilities to handle the difficult aspects of that position. Literacy coaches can build their skills through ongoing training and networking with other coaches. Discussions with others in similar positions can be effective as a means of helping literacy coaches deal with difficult situations.

Guidelines for Success

We believe that certain guidelines for literacy coaches are essential for success. These guidelines come from literacy coaches who have worked successfully with teachers in Literacy Educators Assessing and Developing Early Reading Success (LEADERS), a yearlong professional development program housed at the University of Pittsburgh (Bean, Carroll, & Morris, 2004). These guidelines can help administrators understand the role of the literacy coach and provide the support that coaches need to fulfill their responsibilities.

Using the Teacher's Agenda as a Starting Point

Although there may be specific goals identified by the school as essential for promoting reading achievement, the more that a coach can focus on the needs or goals of the specific teacher, the greater chance there will be of change in classroom practices. For example, if the teacher is especially interested in flexible grouping as a means of providing for students' needs, then the literacy coach can work with the teacher and discuss various ways of introducing flexible grouping into the classroom (e.g., literacy centers, modified scheduling, and so forth) and then assisting the teacher in carrying out the plan. Once that effort is underway, the coach may wish to prompt the teacher to expand his or her thinking about specific literacy strategies such as improving comprehension or incorporating higher quality phonics instruction into classroom practices.

Building Trust

All of the literacy coaches in LEADERS discussed the importance of building a trusting relationship with the teachers. They indicated that it took them several months to develop such a relationship with some teachers, although with others, they developed a relationship much more quickly. Building trust, in their view, was possible because the coaches were able to do the following:

- Be a good listener, willing to hear both professional and personal issues raised by the teacher.
- Demonstrate teaching skills. Teachers were much more responsive—and more willing to admit if they had difficulties (e.g., with classroom management or a particular strategy)—when literacy coaches were willing to model a particular strategy or approach in the classroom.

- Maintain confidentiality. There is little chance of a trusting relationship if teachers think (or know) that the literacy coach is talking about what he or she is seeing in the classroom with others (e.g., administrators, other teachers, and so forth).
- Keep promises. Teachers need to know that the literacy coach will follow through with commitments. Literacy coaches who change plans on a frequent basis or do not arrive as scheduled have little chance of being trusted or valued by teachers.
- Remember that coaching is not an evaluative process. If teachers think that coaches are supervisors or administrators who are making judgments about their teaching, they will be less receptive to the coaching process and less likely to work comfortably with the coach so that change will occur in the classroom.

Working With Students

The literacy coaches in LEADERS indicated that one of the most effective ways of working with teachers was to work with their students. Teachers appreciated the focus on students, especially those with whom they were experiencing difficulty either because students were having trouble learning to read or they exhibited behavior problems. When coaches provided teachers with information about these students, actually worked with them on a short-term basis, and/or listened to teacher concerns about these students, teachers seemed to become more willing to engage in various activities with the coaches. Moreover, when teachers saw that certain strategies or approaches were effective with their students, they tended to become more accepting of using those strategies themselves.

Working with students also creates an environment in which students look forward to and are willing to work with the literacy coach because they have become familiar with the coach in the classroom. This can generate a more collaborative approach to planning for effective reading instruction. Although coaches can—on a short-term basis— work with students, it is essential for these coaches to remember that their primary responsibility is professional development for teachers, and, therefore, teaching students is a means of improving the classroom instruction of teachers.

Modeling Various Approaches and Strategies

Although we have previously noted the value of demonstrating instructional strategies as a means of building trust, we discuss modeling in greater depth here because it is an important procedure for helping teachers understand how a specific activity or strategy should be implemented. Modeling provides teachers with an excellent picture of how they might implement various techniques, an example of how their own students might respond to the techniques, and opportunities for in-depth discussion. It allows teachers to question the coach about certain behaviors or steps. It opens the door for a conversation about teaching and learning. At the same time, we discourage coaches from overusing this approach because the desired outcome is to enable the teacher to actually develop expertise with specific strategies. For example, one district in which we have worked has a policy that if a coach models a lesson for the teacher, within several days the coach should be invited back to see the teacher use the modeled strategy with students.

Recognizing and Accepting Teachers' and Students' Differences

One of the major roles of the literacy coach is helping teachers plan instruction, taking into consideration the individual differences of students. The notion that educators must differentiate instruction to provide for students is certainly a message of Reading First. Such a notion requires educators to accept and appreciate the many differences that exist among students (e.g., instructional needs, cultural diversity, and so forth).

Likewise, literacy coaches must recognize and appreciate the differences that exist among teachers. They must be cognizant of the fact that they will need to work with each teacher in a different manner, depending on each teacher's needs and receptivity. As previously mentioned, literacy coaches might want to begin working with reluctant teachers by providing resources, assisting with assessment, or perhaps modeling a particular strategy or technique. They can work with teachers who are eager to receive feedback about their instruction by visiting their classrooms and reflecting with them about what they see. They also can facilitate the work of the highly effective teacher by supporting them and recognizing their efforts.

Reflecting on One's Performance—An Essential Aspect of the Literacy Coach's Role

Coaching, like teaching, requires that individuals think about what they are doing or have done and how they might improve their performance.

Teachers can reflect on the content that is discussed or presented, the instructional aspects that were shared, or even the processes that were used. Literacy coaches need to take time to think about what went well, what did not go well, and how they might become more effective as they work in schools.

Learning About Coaching

Educators have much to learn about coaching. For example, what are the most valuable activities or roles of coaches? What impact can they have on student performance? Staub and West (2003) indicate that there is no generally accepted coaching model and that specific structures and procedures vary greatly. Goodlad, in a recent interview (as cited in Hall, 2004), identified coaching as a "cottage industry" and called for greater evaluation of coaching efforts in schools. Therefore, it is incumbent on those in leadership roles in the schools to think about their efforts and what they do that they consider to be successful.

By talking with other coaches and principals—that is, forming networks of professionals—coaches can gain insights about their role. Coaches with whom we have talked indicate that the best form of professional development for them has been the opportunity to talk with other coaches. During these discussions, coaches can talk about issues they face and possible solutions. They can describe what they have done that has been successful.

Moreover, coaches, like teachers, will need to get feedback about what they do. They can solicit feedback from teachers by asking them to complete a form indicating which of the coach's activities have been most helpful and by seeking additional ideas from them. The principal also can and should provide feedback that can help the coach perform more effectively. Such feedback, from teachers and principals, should be solicited on a regular basis so literacy coaches can make necessary adjustments or modifications in their role. End-of-the-year feedback is not sufficient. Instead, the principal and coach should sit down together perhaps once a month to discuss the coach's activities and possible goals and plans for the coming month.

Although currently there is not much empirical evidence available about coaching and its impact, there is some literature that provides helpful guidelines for coaches. Coaches and administrators at the school and district levels can use the resources in Table 11.2 to learn more about coaching.

> ● Table 11.2 ●
> ### Resources for Learning About Literacy Coaching
>
> Bean, R.M. (2004). *The reading specialist: Leadership for the classroom, school, and community.* New York: Guilford.
> Dole, J.A. (2004). The changing role of the reading specialist in school reform. *The Reading Teacher, 57*(5), 462–471.
> Lyons, C.A. (2002). Becoming an effective literacy coach: What does it take? In E.M. Rodgers & G.S. Pinnell (Eds.), *Learning from teaching in literacy education: New perspectives on professional development* (pp. 93–118). Portsmouth, NH: Heinemann.
> Lyons, C.A., & Pinnell, G.S. (2001). *Systems for change in literacy education: A guide to professional development.* Portsmouth, NH: Heinemann.
> Walpole, S., & McKenna, M.C. (2004). *The literacy coach's handbook: A guide to research-based practice.* New York: Guilford.

Conclusion

The growing trend to employ literacy coaches in schools as an approach for improving classroom instruction demands that principals and others in leadership positions have an excellent idea of what coaches can—and cannot—do. Administrators must be aware of the knowledge, skills, and dispositions that quality literacy coaches need to possess and be willing to work with coaches, especially in the beginning of the program, to create an environment that is conducive to coaching as a means of improving classroom practices. Ideas from coaches who have been in the field provide key insights that will enable the newly employed coach to begin with a clearer picture of what the role requires and how he or she can most effectively work with teachers. Coaching puts the emphasis on personnel because quality teaching can make a difference for students.

REFERENCES

Bean, R., Carroll, K., & Morris, J. (2004, April). *Role of literacy coaches in promoting teacher change.* Paper presented at the American Educational Research Association, San Diego, CA.

Cooter, R.B. (2003). Teacher "capacity-building" helps urban children succeed. *The Reading Teacher, 57*(2), 198–205.

Darling-Hammond, L., & McLaughlin, M.W. (1995). Policies that support professional development in an era of reform. *Phi Delta Kappan, 76*(8), 597–604.

Hall, B. (2004). Literacy coaches: An evolving role. *Carnegie Reporter, 3*(1), 10–19.

International Reading Association. (2003). *Standards for reading professionals—Revised 2003.* Newark, DE: Author.

International Reading Association. (2004). *The role and qualifications of the reading coach in the United States* (Position statement). Newark, DE: Author.

Joyce, B., & Showers, B. (1995). *Student achievement through staff development: Fundamentals of school renewal*. White Plains, NY: Longman.

Joyce, B., & Showers, B. (2002). *Student achievement through staff development* (3rd ed.). Alexandria, VA: Association for Supervision and Curriculum Development.

National Commission on Teaching and America's Future. (1996). *What matters most: Teaching for America's future*. New York: Teachers College Press.

No Child Left Behind Act of 2001, Pub. L. No. 107-110, 115 Stat. 1425 (2002). Retrieved October 1, 2005, from http://edworkforce.house.gov/issues/107th/education/nclb/nclb.htm

Staub, F., & West, L. (2003). *Content-focused coaching: Transforming mathematics lessons*. Portsmouth, NH: Heinemann.

CHAPTER 12

Revitalizing the Literacy Program: A Work in Progress at One Elementary School

Martha A. Colwell and Sherry L. Alleman

KELLY AND JOELLE team teach a third-grade special education inclusion classroom. They begin their mystery genre study with the whole class on the rug for an interactive read-aloud. Joelle, the inclusion teacher, introduces the book and asks for predictions. She then reads the story while demonstrating fluency and modeling comprehension strategies. She solicits predictions and encourages vocabulary development. Kelly, the general education teacher, surveys the class and joins in when appropriate. A follow-up discussion includes characteristics of the genre. Next, the class completes a graphic organizer of mystery criteria on chart paper.

Using leveled readers, the class continues to investigate the mystery genre during small-group focused instruction. (These groups have been determined by assessments.) Both teachers meet with a small group at opposite ends of the room. While students read independently, each teacher completes individual conferences where children read aloud and discuss the comprehension strategies they used. During the independent portion of the small-group explicit instruction, the teachers have students use sticky notes to identify clues about what will happen next based on their inferences and locate vocabulary that adds to the development and interest in the story. Both teachers take running records and keep anecdotal notes of students' performance. Then, the small group reconvenes to discuss the inferences and new vocabulary words students found in the reading. Meanwhile, the rest of the students complete literacy center activities focused on word study and comprehension strategies. Independent activities include reading more mysteries, completing new graphic organizers, adding new words to their vocabulary notebooks, and completing a poster pamphlet about their favorite mystery.

The literacy block in Kelly and Joelle's classroom is one example of the evolution in the literacy program that can take place at any school. It does not happen overnight, and change will need to continue. Similar to the rock cycle in geology, comprehensive literacy development involves evolution and change in order to reach its goal—in this case, the goal of improving literacy instruction for *all* students.

Administrators at all levels need to stay current in their knowledge regarding effective reading instruction, which necessitates an understanding of the findings of the National Reading Panel Report of 2000 (National Institute of Child Health and Human Development), the No Child Left Behind Act of 2001 (2002), and subsequent Reading First regulations as well as scientific research, terminology, best literacy practices, and assessment analyses. This knowledge will help ensure that school staffs possess the necessary resources within their own schools in terms of time, professional development, and materials necessary for effective reading instruction so that, indeed, no child is left behind.

In this chapter, we explain how an elementary school can revitalize its literacy program to better meet today's demands for education and align with requirements for Reading First and other literacy standards found in state curriculum frameworks. The journey may not be easy, especially in the beginning, and it will require time, as well as philosophical, behavioral, and physical changes for all educators.

Developing a Shared Literacy Vision

The journey toward developing a comprehensive literacy program should begin with administrators leading the development of a shared vision. It is critical that administrators without a strong background in literacy expertise forge a relationship with a knowledgeable core group on the staff, most likely comprised of reading specialists, literacy coaches, and classroom teachers current in their knowledge of best literacy practices. The administrator should select a literacy coach or leader to help develop and lead the literacy vision, one who has the knowledge of best practices in reading instruction based on scientific research, an understanding of legislative issues, and the respect of the staff. The literacy vision must be supported by central office administrators, building-level principals, school committee members, and all staff members and viewed as a beacon guiding the way to the development of a comprehensive literacy program (Baron, 1999; Reutzel & Cooter, 2003). Finally, administrators need to routinely walk through classrooms and conduct both formal and informal observations to determine whether the instruction being implemented is based on the identified vision. This observation data also can be used to help administrators monitor the amount and type of instruction occurring in key areas of reading, including phonemic awareness, phonics, fluency, vocabulary, comprehension, oral language, writing, and so forth.

Realities and Strategies for Improving Literacy Instruction

Every school has its own personality, expertise, and needs. These school-specific characteristics make each journey toward improving the comprehensive literacy program unique; however, certain aspects of the transformation can be adapted or copied because there are definitive realities and strategies for improving literacy instruction. These realities might serve as signposts to help make the journey to revitalize the literacy program successful.

Reality #1: Administrators at All Levels Must Serve as Catalysts for Change

The shared literacy vision and subsequent expectations sparked by the administrator and literacy leadership team require continued professional development, discussion, and ongoing support. Financial resources and time for professional development in best literacy practices that are based on scientific research will enable teachers to easily provide explicit instruction in phonemic awareness, phonics, vocabulary, comprehension, fluency, oral language development, and writing. Without administrators who understand and plan for ongoing professional development, schoolwide change in literacy practices will not occur. Administrators must ensure that every classroom has the staff and resources to meet the needs of the shared literacy vision.

In addition to financial support for resources, equipment, and supplies that promote best literacy practices, administrators must set the expectation for the creation of classroom environments that promote literacy development. This type of classroom environment may vary greatly from more traditional classrooms. Administrators play a major role in helping teachers recognize the need for changing the physical environment as well as the format for instruction. The following classroom description reflects how physical surroundings help create a literate environment.

> The first things noticed by someone entering Robyn's third-grade inclusion classroom are the instructional areas designed to invite students into the learning environment. There is a centrally displayed work board that lists the schedule of activities for the day for each student group. (The schedule changes daily, but routines stay intact.) There are student cubbyholes for storing individual supplies, a large rug for daily class meetings and whole-class instruction, an easel to hold chart paper, a horseshoe-shaped table for small-group instruction, and colorful student desks and tables in various arrangements for working together on projects. In addition to a word wall, there are charts that display comprehension strategies, pocket charts for practice with phonics, and many samples of poetry that encourage phonemic awareness. The room is filled with books: There is a large, organized classroom library with texts from many genres to interest and challenge every student; a special literature display area near the rug to reflect the current genre study; and a listening center with audiobooks to increase students' fluency. There are centers around the perimeter of the room to promote independent reading practice, word study, and the integration of content area subjects, and there is also a computer area to incorporate technology with literacy.

Robyn's classroom environment illustrates her commitment to developing a comprehensive literacy program that includes whole-class direct instruction in reading and writing, small-group guided practice, and individual application of whole-class lessons. Through school-based professional development organized and supported by the principal and her own extensive reading of professional development texts, Robyn has learned how to develop a classroom environment that supports the shared literacy vision.

Reality #2: The Evolution Toward a Literacy Program That Supports All Learners Is a Slow Process

After studying the development of effective literacy programs, Lipson (2002) states that it often takes 8–10 years to develop a coherent literacy program. To facilitate this process, Administrators should interview all staff using the same questions to determine individual viewpoints regarding what works and what does not in their literacy program (e.g., books and materials) and to determine the staff members' current level of understanding of literacy strategies and processes. Using this information, administrators can organize study groups to develop a vision for the school and an action plan for implementing it. High expectations for each student must be the guiding light for all visions (Maine Department of Education, 2000).

Teaching teams can help serve as the basis for change. Each team should be composed of three to five classroom teachers, a literacy coach and/or a reading specialist, a special education teacher, and possibly an instructional assistant. Administrators can help arrange the school schedule to give each team common planning time to prepare curriculum maps, design instructional units, review assessment results, and plan instruction. Teams also can pilot new materials and work on budgets. Working together, teachers can implement the shared literacy vision. Administrators should meet with team leaders on a monthly basis to hear and discuss team concerns.

The following example illustrates how literacy coaches can provide ongoing professional development to meet the individual needs of the staff. It also demonstrates the notion that new strategies should be implemented in a manner that allows numerous application opportunities before moving to a new focus area. Teachers are more comfortable implementing new strategies with this type of ongoing support, which takes time to implement fully.

Team 6, composed of four classroom teachers, a literacy coach, a reading specialist, one special education teacher, and one instructional assistant, meets during their common planning time. The focus of this meeting is implementing literature circles in third grade. Andrea, the literacy coach, reviews the basic roles for students to assume during literature discussions. She has samples of chapter books in the realistic fiction genre on a variety of levels. Each member of the team selects appropriate titles to ensure success for all students in the classroom. Then the team discusses the idea of creating student notebooks for evaluation of comprehension strategies and vocabulary development. Finally, the team plans to meet with administrators to request resources so they can implement their plan. The team, under the leadership of the literacy coach, focuses on changing from a model of one-size-fits-all instruction to one that recognizes the need for differentiated instruction to meet individual student needs. One teacher on the team states, "Our principal and our literacy coach [are taking] us into the 21st century. They [are giving] us the knowledge, support, and confidence to implement a well-rounded literacy program in our classrooms."

The team's focus on implementing new instructional strategies such as literature circles and differentiated instruction took several years to develop. Thus, it is important for administrators to recognize that staff will have varying levels of knowledge, expertise, and confidence. They must recognize the need for flexibility when they and literacy coaches work with teachers on planning, implementing, and modeling a new teaching strategy. Professional development and coaching support must match the needs of the teachers and will vary in the length of time necessary for sustained implementation. Most teachers will require several years of practical experience and professional development before they feel completely comfortable with instructional change.

Reality #3: Professional Development in All Areas of Implementation Is Necessary

Joyce and Showers (1995) state that teachers require sustained professional development before they can fully implement new instructional designs. The following vignette exemplifies the result of ongoing professional development in differentiating phonics instruction based on the students' needs. Charla, a special education teacher, took an online early intervention course in reading and incorporated many of the ideas into the literacy block for her 13 third-grade students who were reading on a first-grade level. This course helped Charla understand the purpose and rationale behind the concepts and strategies that are necessary to develop students' phonemic awareness and phonics skills.

Charla is meeting with a group of four students who share similar levels of phonological development, as determined by classroom assessments. The focus for the lesson is phonemic segmentation through the use of plastic letters and Elkonin boxes (Elkonin, 1973) whereby students demonstrate their ability to segment sounds within a word by pushing a letter into a marked box as they hear each sound within the word. (Charla uses this type of lesson with Elkonin boxes daily.) Charla draws Elkonin boxes on paper; they will be used to isolate and record sounds during a 3–5 minute activity. (Elkonin boxes can be used one on one or in small skill groups.)

Charla begins by reading the first word that the group will segment, *play*. Charla also places blank boxes in front of the students.

Charla: How many sounds do you hear in this word?
Thomas: Three.
Charla: (selects three blank boxes) What letters will we put in the first box?
Susan: P.
Charla: (places a *p* in the first box) What will we put in the second box?
James: A.
Charla: (very slowly) P-l-ay. What have we missed?
Carol: L.
(Charla removes the *a* and places an *l* in the second box. [If this were a digraph, she would have placed both letters in the first box.])
Charla: What belongs in the third box?
Thomas: A.
Charla: In this word, the sound /ā/ is made by two letters, *a* and *y*. (She places the letter *y* in the box with *a*.)
Charla: What other words have the ending sound /ā/ and are spelled *ay*?
Carol: Day.
James: Stay.

The students in this group then begin to read a story in pairs while Charla takes a running record of Carol's reading of the text.

By reading a story after working with Elkonin boxes, Charla provides her students with the opportunity to use their segmenting skills to decode words in a real situation. Then Charla can assess her students' ability to apply this strategy to their reading.

Another option for professional development that moves beyond one-time inservice training for individual teachers is to provide intensive staff development for one teacher or a group of teachers on the focus skill or strategy. These teachers will in turn train the remaining teachers on the same skill. This train-the-trainers model can be implemented to extend new learning to all members of the staff. For example, all team literacy coaches at the elementary school receive a day of professional development in how to execute running records of students' oral reading. The literacy coaches then provide professional development to their fellow team members on the same topic. Teams continue to meet until all members feel proficient in administering running records.

Reality #4: Assessment Informs Instruction

Administrators cannot just provide teachers with required materials or professional development materials and expect to get good results.

Teachers, like students, are unique in their professional development needs. In addition to learning about instruction, topics for professional development also should include administration and analysis of various types of assessments teachers can use to inform their instruction, measure individual student achievement, and evaluate program effectiveness. Classroom literacy assessments should be comprehensive and include oral reading, fluency, comprehension, and writing.

After implementing a comprehensive literacy assessment program, administrators should set up a system for collecting schoolwide data with these same assessment tools. The results of this data collection then should be used to set literacy goals with individual teachers and goals for the school—both benchmark goals and long-range goals. It is important that administrators follow up by collecting and reviewing subsequent assessment data to determine how well the school is doing regarding the established benchmarks. Finally, administrators can use this information to provide support where it is most needed in the school and make changes where necessary to ensure success with the Reading First program. The following vignette illustrates how a team of educators worked together to evaluate assessment data for the purpose of planning future instruction.

> During their common planning time, Lynn and Chuck, two classroom teachers; Eric, a special education teacher; and Roberta, a reading specialist, meet to discuss the assessment results for two classes of third-grade students. The focus of their meeting is to establish instructional groups based on common areas of need determined by their analysis of students' test results in comprehension, fluency, oral reading, and phonics. By the end of the 45-minute meeting, they have selected instructional groups, developed a schedule for intervention, and established an instructional plan for struggling readers.

Reality #5: The Comprehensive Literacy Program Requires a Seamless Intervention Program for Struggling Readers

Analyzing assessments provides administrators and teachers with timely evidence for identifying all students who need intervention services. An intervention program should be implemented throughout the school for all struggling readers, which can include regular education students, special education students, or English-language learners (ELLs). A seamless approach to intervention will enable each student in need of additional instruction in the essential elements of literacy to receive intervention services. Administrators must establish the expectation that explicit, focused intervention will be scheduled for all identified students. A seamless approach means that staff development must be provided for all staff members responsible for implementing the intervention services. To facilitate this approach, intervention providers can include reading specialists, literacy coaches, classroom teachers, special education teachers, ELL program staff, and highly qualified teaching assistants working under the supervision of a literacy coach or leader.

The following vignette depicts a seamless approach to intervention. This scenario easily could have taken place in a regular classroom or a special education inclusion room because a successful intervention program emphasizes the same characteristics as a comprehensive literacy program, including explicit instruction in phonemic awareness, phonics, vocabulary, fluency, comprehension, oral language, and writing.

Stevany's ELL class is composed of 17 second-grade students with diverse cultures and languages but all in need of additional reading instruction. Although similar in physical appearance to other literacy classrooms, the classroom has fewer students and additional bins of children's literature in other languages. The intervention program takes place in the classroom during the literacy block. The groups rotate every half hour so at the end of the 90-minute literacy block, each student has had an explicit lesson focusing on strategies related to fluency, vocabulary development, comprehension, and other identified areas of need, in addition to independent time at learning centers.

Five students are working at literacy centers, completing a variety of tasks as outlined on the work board, while six other students meet with Stevany. This second group is rehearsing a Readers Theatre script that they will perform for the class at the end of the week. The focus of this group is oral comprehension of text as expressed in fluency, phrasing, and facial expression. The remaining six students are at one end of the room with Sherry, the reading specialist, receiving intervention services that incorporate reading strategies such as predicting, questioning, clarifying, and summarizing. Today's intervention lesson is the first day of reading the informational book *Baby Whales Drink Milk* (Esbensen, 1994). The book is introduced via a discussion on mammals where connections are made between human babies and baby whales. The students then begin to predict the similarities and differences between fish and whales. Sherry introduces vocabulary words during the discussion. The stage has now been set to begin silent reading. The techniques of reciprocal teaching (Palincsar & Brown, 1984) are evident as students use sticky notes to list unknown vocabulary or confusing information. Discussion includes clarification of items on the sticky notes, personal connections to the passage, and predictions for future sections.

Administrators need to recognize that intervention should be in addition to a comprehensive classroom literacy program. Therefore, administrators should be sure to work with classroom teachers and intervention staff to establish schedules promoting optimum instructional times for classroom literacy and intervention.

Conclusion

Knowledgeable administrators who work hand in hand with literacy coaches and classroom teachers to provide appropriate and effective reading instruction create schools that are student centered—that is, discussions and decisions are based on what is best for students. As teachers refine their literacy teaching skills, their individuality and creativity are able to emerge, yet a common thread of incorporating best literacy practices is still evident. Teachers continue to experience professional growth, implement various strategies and techniques, and experiment with classroom configurations.

Even when reading achievement improves, however, the journey does not end. Teaching and learning is a continuous cycle. Administrators need to reevaluate teachers' and students' performance at regularly defined intervals. As with most cycles, best practices in literacy continue to evolve, and better techniques and strategies constantly are created to meet students' everchanging needs. Since the changes to the comprehensive literacy program began at this elementary school, the student population has changed, which means more support is needed for ELLs. Adapting to the needs of the new student populations, implementing current state and federal legislative mandates, and accounting for students' constantly changing areas of strength and weakness require change to be a constant factor in the revitalization of the literacy program at this elementary school and all schools.

REFERENCES

Baron, J.B. (1999). *Exploring high and improving reading achievement in Connecticut.* Washington, DC: U.S. Department of Education.

Elkonin, D.B. (1973). USSR. In J.A. Downing (Ed.), *Comparative reading: Cross-national study of behavior and processes in reading and writing* (pp. 551–580). New York: Macmillan.

Joyce, B., & Showers, B. (1995). *Student achievement through staff development: Fundamentals of school renewal.* White Plains, NY: Longman.

Lipson, M.J. (2002). *Creating success one school at a time: Taking responsibility for our own destiny.* Paper presented at the Massachusetts Reading Conference, Sturbridge, MA.

Maine Department of Education, Center for Inquiry on Literacy. (2000). *A solid foundation: Supportive contexts for early literacy programs in Maine schools.* Augusta, ME: Author.

National Institute of Child Health and Human Development. (2000). *Report of the National Reading Panel. Teaching children to read: An evidence-based assessment of the scientific research literature on reading and its implications for reading instruction* (NIH Publication No. 00-4769). Washington, DC: U.S. Government Printing Office.

No Child Left Behind Act of 2001, Pub. L. No. 107-110, 115 Stat. 1425 (2002). Retrieved October 1, 2005, from http://edworkforce.house.gov/issues/107th/education/nclb/nclb.htm

Palincsar, A.S., & Brown, A.L. (1984). Reciprocal teaching of comprehension-fostering and comprehension-monitoring activities. *Cognition and Instruction, 2,* 117–175.

Reutzel, D.R., & Cooter, R.D., Jr. (2003). *Strategies for reading assessment and instruction* (2nd ed.). Upper Saddle River, NJ: Merrill Prentice Hall.

LITERATURE CITED

Esbensen, B.J. (1994). *Baby whales drink milk.* Boston: Houghton Mifflin.

CONCLUSION

Carrice Cummins

Improving reading achievement for all students is an awesome goal for schools to attempt to achieve. The No Child Left Behind Act of 2001 (NCLB; 2002) and subsequent Reading First legislation consistently refer to the need for highly qualified teachers to implement the explicit and systematic teaching of reading. However, this alone is not enough. Successful implementation also requires that administrators be knowledgeable of issues concerning reading instruction and actively involved in the teaching and learning occurring within their schools and districts.

Throughout this volume, the concept of administrators working as leaders in literacy instruction has been emphasized. Leadership expertise generally falls on a continuum, with each administrator possessing some degree of expertise at each target point between change agent and instructional leader. It is crucial that administrators examine their places along the continuum to do what good leaders do: Assess the situation, develop a plan, and begin the process of narrowing the gap between the outer ranges of expertise. The challenge for administrators is not only to become knowledgeable of current literacy issues and effective components of teaching reading but also to be able to integrate this knowledge with sound managerial skills. This combined action will enhance teacher support and ultimately bring about increased student achievement.

This volume began as a way to support administrators in their endeavors to move from primarily being managers or change agents at the school to being instructional leaders capable of teaching and learning with their teachers. It is the hope of the editor and contributors that this volume helps serve as a starting point for building essential background knowledge and providing sound strategies that can be implemented in classrooms immediately, while opening the door to more detailed investigations into key areas of instruction outlined in NCLB and Reading First—phonemic awareness, phonics, vocabulary, fluency, and comprehension—as well as the areas of oral language development, writing, motivation, working with struggling readers, and understanding the roles of literacy coaches. This knowledge not only will assist administrators in observing sound reading practices but, more importantly, also will help them make strong instructional decisions regarding implementation of reading programs, strategies, and practices that are tailored to the specific needs of the school and district populations.

Teaching children to read is a challenging responsibility. Fulfilling this responsibility requires the knowledge and guidance not only of teachers but of all educators involved in planning, developing, implementing, and overseeing the instructional program. The time is now for administrators to make the move from being managers to being instructional leaders who understand literacy issues and the importance of supporting teachers in their endeavors to provide sound literacy instruction for all students.

Teachers and administrators armed with understandings about the "what," "when," and "how to" of reading instruction combine the art and science of teaching reading, which is powerful. As previously identified by Barth (1990), a good school involves everyone working together. Teaching and learning together can make a difference in students' reading achievement, but it requires a well-rounded administrator—someone who is a great manager, a positive change agent, and a knowledgeable literacy advocate.

REFERENCES

Barth, R. (1990). A personal vision of a good school. *Phi Delta Kappan, 71*, 512–516.
No Child Left Behind Act of 2001, Pub. L. No. 107-110, 115 Stat. 1425 (2002). Retrieved October 1, 2005, from http://edworkforce.house.gov/issues/107th/education/nclb/nclb.htm

AUTHOR INDEX

A

Abbott, R.D., 107
Abbott, S.P., 107
Adams, M.J., 20
Afflerbach, P., 75, 82, 85, 134
Ahrens, M.G., 122
Allington, R.L., 13, 16, 119–122, 128, 132–136
Almasi, J., 123
Almasi, J.F., 133
Anderman, E.M., 120
Anderson, R.C., 44, 46, 122
Armbruster, B.B., 20, 32–34
Artley, S.A., 123
Asselin, M., 44

B

Baker, L., 75
Bamman, H.A., 47
Bandura, A., 120
Barbaranelli, C., 120
Baron, J.B., 155
Barth, R.S., 1, 165
Bean, R.M., 147, 151
Beatty, A.S., 62
Beck, I.L., 44–48, 94
Beeler, T., 20
Bell, K.M., 131
Benson, V., 98, 101
Berglund, R.L., 49
Berninger, V.W., 107
Betts, E.A., 131
Bickart, T.S., 97
Biemiller, A., 44
Blachowicz, C.L.Z., 49, 56
Blasé, J., 10–11, 13
Block, C.C., 73–78, 80, 85
Booth, D., 13, 15
Boyd-Zaharias, J., 134
Brassell, D., 44, 48, 50–53, 55
Brett, J., 31
Britton, J., 93
Brock, C., 44
Brophy, J., 119
Brown, A.L., 161
Bruner, J.S., 95
Bryk, A.S., 134
Burke, C., 100
Burns, M.S., 103

C

Caffey, P., 28
Cain-Thoreson, C., 75, 82
Calfee, R.C., 48
Calkins, L.M., 92–93
Cambourne, B., 119
Camilli, G., 133
Campbell, J.R., 62, 123
Campbell, R., 92, 98, 101
Caprara, G., 120
Carnine, D.W., 44
Carroll, K., 147
Cawelti, G., 15
Celano, D., 120
Chall, J., 74, 76
Chard, D.J., 62, 134
Cherry, M.T., 90, 96
Christie, J., 21, 23, 27
Codling, R.M., 123
Coles, G., 128
Collins, C., 74, 76
Combs, M., 100
Cooter, R.B., 120, 140
Cooter, R.D., Jr., 155
Coyle, G., 44
Cronbach, L.J., 48
Cullinan, B.E., 96
Cummins, C., 98, 101
Cunningham, A.E., 20, 45, 121–122
Cunningham, J.W., 54, 128
Cunningham, P., 129
Cunningham, P.M., 13, 16, 34–35, 38, 54, 119, 133

D

D'Agostino, J.V., 133
Dale, E., 47–48
Darling-Hammond, L., 140
Darrow, L., 28
Deal, T.E., 10
Deford, D.E., 134
Dickinson, D.K., 91
Dodge, D.T., 97
Dole, J.A., 151
Drum, P.A., 48
Duffelmeyer, F.A., 56
Duffy, G.G., 133
Duffy-Hester, A., 34
Durkin, D., 76

N

NAGY, W.E., 44, 46, 48, 122
NATION, P., 47
NATIONAL COMMISSION ON TEACHING AND
   AMERICA'S FUTURE, 140
NATIONAL INSTITUTE FOR LITERACY, 128, 130
NATIONAL INSTITUTE OF CHILD HEALTH AND
   HUMAN DEVELOPMENT (NICHD), 3, 14, 19,
   21, 27–28, 32, 43, 57, 62, 74, 78, 91, 106,
   109, 114, 117, 128, 154
NEUMAN, S.B., 120
NICHOLS, W.D., 57
NO CHILD LEFT BEHIND (NCLB) ACT, 1–2, 8,
   19, 32, 43, 57, 62, 73, 91, 117, 128, 140,
   154, 164
NOWAK, R., 136

O

O'CONNOR, R.E., 131
OGLE, D., 52
OLDFATHER, P., 123
OMANSON, R., 75
O'ROURKE, J., 47
OSBORN, J., 20, 32–34
OSHIRO, M., 111

P

PADAK, N.D., 67–68
PALINCSAR, A.S., 161
PALMER, B.M., 123
PARIS, S.G., 75, 77
PASTORELLI, C., 120
PATE-BAIN, H., 134
PEARSON, P.D., 74, 77
PEKRUN, R., 118
PETERSON, K.D., 10
PETERSON, R.I., 95
PIKULSKI, J.J., 16, 62
PINNELL, G.S., 62, 134, 151
PITTLEMAN, S.D., 49
PRESSLEY, M., 75–76, 82, 85
PRIOR, J., 23
PURCELL-GATES, V., 91

R

RASINSKI, T.V., 62–64, 67–69
REUTZEL, D.R., 120, 155
RICHARDS, T., 107
RISLEY, T.R., 44, 91, 93
RODGERS, L., 73, 76–77, 80
ROSER, N., 65
ROSKOS, K.A., 92–93
ROSWELL, J., 13, 15
ROUTMAN, R., 98
ROWAN, B., 134
RUBIN, P.M., 134
RUPLEY, W.H., 57

S

SACKOR, S.M., 131
SCHAUF, J., 28
SCHIEFELE, U., 121
SCHUNK, D.H., 119
SCHWARTZ, D.M., 54
SCOTT, J.A., 44, 48
SELTZER, M., 134

SENDAK, M., 48
SEUSS, DR., 26
SHANAHAN, T., 91, 107, 114, 129–130, 134
SHANKWEILER, D., 29
SHEARER, B., 131
SHORT, J.C., 100
SHORT, K., 98
SHORT, R., 131
SHOWERS, B., 140, 158
SLATER, M.H., 44
SLAVIN, R.E., 134
SLOAN, G.D., 103
SNOW, C.E., 91, 103
SOLIC, K.J., 127, 132
SPAULDING, C.L., 121
SPECTOR, J.E., 29
STAHL, A., 34
STAHL, S.A., 32–35, 62
STANOVICH, K.E., 18, 20, 28, 45, 121–122
STAUB, F., 150
STEWART, M.T., 101
STRECKER, S., 65
STRICKLAND, D.S., 96
STURTEVANT, E., 67–68

T

TABORS, P.O., 92–93
TAYLOR, B., 131
TAYLOR, B.M., 122
TEALE, W.H., 33
TIERNEY, R.J., 107, 114
TOPPING, K., 65
TRABASSO, T., 75
TRACEY, D.H., 33
TRELEASE, J., 97, 100
TURNER, J., 75, 77
TYLER, B., 62

V

VARGAS, S., 133
VAUGHN, S., 62, 134
VUKELICH, C., 21, 27
VYGOTSKY, E., 48

W

WADE, B., 98
WALPOLE, S., 151
WARREN, R., 75
WASIK, B.A., 75, 77, 134
WEST, L., 150
WHITELEY, C., 76, 85
WIGFIELD, A., 118–119
WILHELM, J.D., 133
WILSON, R.M., 121
WIXSON, K.K., 62

X–Z

XU, S., 23
YOPP, H.K., 20–21, 25
YURECKO, M., 133
ZEIG, J.L., 127, 132
ZIGMOND, N., 131
ZIMMERMAN, B.J., 119
ZIMMERMANN, S., 75
ZMACH, C., 127, 132
ZUTTELL, J.B., 62

SUBJECT INDEX

Page numbers followed by *t* or *f* indicate tables or figures, respectively.

FDL. *See* Fluency Development Lesson
FLUENCY, 3, 60–71; administrators and, 68–69;
assessment of, 63–64, 63*t*, 69; definition
of, 61–63; synergistic instruction in,
66–68; teaching, 64–69
FLUENCY DEVELOPMENT LESSON (FDL), 67–68

G–I

GRAND CONVERSATIONS, 95
HIERARCHICAL ARRAY CHARTS, 52, 53*f*, 112*f*
INDEPENDENT READING: time for, 122–123
INFERENTIAL COMPREHENSION, 75; lesson on,
82–83
INITIAL CONSONANTS: blending, 37–38; sounds,
36–37
INQUIRY SESSIONS, 95–96
INSTRUCTIONAL LEADER: term, 8–9; in today's
school, 10–13
INSTRUCTIONAL LEADERSHIP: and achievement,
16; steps to, 10
INSTRUCTIONAL RESOURCE: administrators as, 13
INTERVENTION PROGRAM FOR STRUGGLING READERS:
in comprehensive literacy program,
160–162; design of, 127–138

J–K

JOURNALS: and motivation, 117
KENNEDY, JOHN F., 9
K-W-L PLUS, 52–54, 55*f*

L

LEADERS. *See* Literacy Educators Assessing
and Developing Early Reading Success
LEADERS: instructional, 8–13; teacher, 12–13
LEADERSHIP: administrators and, 7–17;
instructional, 10, 16; literacy, 2–4;
management and, 9–10
LEARNING: administrators and, 1–2
LETTER–SOUND RELATIONS, 34
LIBRARY: administrator's, 13
LITERACY COACHES, 139–152; duties of,
141–144, 142*t*–143*t*; guidelines for,
147–150; professional development for,
150, 151*t*; and reading program, 157–158;
sample job description for, 145*f*;
selection of, 144–146
LITERACY EDUCATION: administrators and,
vii–viii, 1–6, 13, 164–165; improvement
of, strategies for, 155–162; revitalizing,
153–163. *See also* reading instruction;
reading program
LITERACY EDUCATORS ASSESSING AND
DEVELOPING EARLY READING SUCCESS
(LEADERS), 147
LITERACY LEADERSHIP: administrators and, 2;
need for, 2–4
LITERACY VISION: shared, development of,
154–156
LITERAL COMPREHENSION, 75

M

MANAGEMENT: and leadership, 9–10
MAP INSTRUCTION, 64–66
METACOGNITIVE COMPREHENSION, 75–76
MINI-INTERVENTIONS, 83–85
MODELING: fluency, 64; literacy coaches and,
148–149
MONITORING STRATEGY, 129, 129*t*
MOTIVATION, 4, 116–126; expectancy-value
theory of, 118–119; importance of, 118;
questions on, 119–124

N

NO CHILD LEFT BEHIND (NCLB) ACT: and
leadership role of administrators, 7–17;
on literacy leadership, 2
NONSTOP PAPERS, 107–109

O

ONSETS, 26–28
OPENNESS: and achievement, 15
ORAL LANGUAGE, 3–4, 90–105; emphasis on,
rationale for, 91–92; instructional
strategies, 92–98; and vocabulary
development, 44–45, 52–56
ORAL READING FLUENCY ASSESSMENT, 63–64, 63*t*

P

PARAPROFESSIONALS: and struggling readers,
134
PARENTS: and fluency, 69; and oral language,
91–93
PART B OF NO CHILD LEFT BEHIND ACT. *See*
Reading First Initiative
PERFORMANCE STRATEGIES: for vocabulary
instruction, 56
PERSONALIZED INSTRUCTION: for struggling
readers, 132–134
PHONEMES, 21
PHONEMIC AWARENESS, 3, 18–30; definition of,
19–20; versus phonics, 19–20; and
reading development, 20; teaching,
20–28
PHONICS, 3, 31–41; definition of, 32–33;
versus phonemic awareness, 19–20; for
struggling readers, 128; teaching, 33–40;
using to figure out words, 38–39
PICTURE SOUND SORTS, 24*f*
PRACTICE: and fluency, 65–66; and struggling
readers, 130–131
PRINCIPALS. *See* administrators
PRINT: environmental, 21, 22*f*; exposure to,
and vocabulary development, 44–45
PROFESSIONAL DEVELOPMENT, 140;
administrators and, 11; and reading
program, 158–159
PURPOSE: and comprehension, lesson on,
82–83

Q–R

QUICK SHARE, 123
READ-ALOUDS: and oral language, 97–98; planning, 98–103, 99*f*; template for, 102*f*; term, 97; time for, 123–124; for vocabulary instruction, 48
READER RESPONSE JOURNAL, 117
READERS THEATRE, 65
READING FIRST INITIATIVE, 2–3; on comprehension, 73–74; on fluency, 62; on motivation, 117; purposes of, 8; and writing, 106–107
READING INSTRUCTION: administrator knowledge on, 14–15; components of, 3; effective, elements of, 3–4, 14; on phonemic awareness, 20–28. *See also* literacy education
READING MATERIALS: and motivation, 120–121
READING PROGRAM: evaluation of, 14–15; revitalizing, 153–163; term, 3; time frame for, 156–158
READING VOLUME: and struggling readers, 130–131
REFLECTION: literacy coaches and, 149–150
REPEATED READINGS: and fluency, 65–66
RESEARCH-BASED COMPREHENSION INSTRUCTION, 72–89; definition of, 73–76
RESPONSIBILITY: of administrators, 9
RETELLING, 101
RHYME, 25–26
RIMES, 26–28
ROLE PLAY, 100–101

S

SCAFFOLDING: administrators and, 2; for comprehension instruction, 78–79
SCAVENGER HUNTS, 54–56
SCHEDULE. *See* time
SCHOOLS: achieving, characteristics of, 15–16; demographics, and comprehension instruction, 73
SCIENTIFIC RESEARCH-BASED READING PROGRAMS, 128; comprehension instruction in, 72–89; NCLB on, 3, 8; for struggling readers, 127–138
SEMANTIC FEATURE ANALYSIS GRIDS, 52, 52*f*
SEMANTIC MAPS, 49–51, 50*f*
SKETCH TO STRETCH, 100
SOUND ISOLATION, 21–25
SPECIAL EDUCATION STUDENTS. *See* struggling readers
SPELLING: and phonics instruction, 34–35
STORY MAPS, 109–111, 110*f*
STRICKLAND, DOROTHY S., vii–viii
STRUGGLING READERS: intervention for, design of, 127–138; reading program and, 160–162
STUDENT READING SKILLS IMPROVEMENT GRANTS. *See* Reading First Initiative

STUDENT-TO-TEACHER READER RESPONSE JOURNAL, 117
SUMMARIES, 111–113, 113*f*
SYNERGISTIC FLUENCY INSTRUCTION, 66–68
SYNTHETIC PHONICS INSTRUCTION, 34

T

TALK, 93–96; and vocabulary development, 52–56. *See also* oral language
TAPR. *See* teachers as professional readers
TEACHER LEADERS: development of, 12–13
TEACHERS: administrators and, 12; literacy coaches and, 146–147
TEACHERS AS PROFESSIONAL READERS (TAPR): study groups, 133
TEACHING: administrators and, 1–2
TEACHING TEAMS: and reading program, 157–158
TEAMWORK: and achievement, 15
TEXT SELECTION: for read-alouds, 98; for struggling readers, 131–132; student opportunities for, 121; student support for, 121–122
THINK-ALOUDS, 78, 81–82
THINKING GUIDES, 80–81
TIME: for comprehension instruction, 74; for independent reading, 122–123; literacy coaches and, 144; for literacy program evolution, 156–158; for read-alouds and book sharing, 123–124; for vocabulary instruction, 57
TRANSACTIONAL STRATEGY INSTRUCTION: for comprehension, 76
TRUST: literacy coaches and, 147–148
TUTORING: for struggling readers, 134

V

VENN DIAGRAM, 111, 112*f*
VERY SMALL GROUP INTERVENTIONS: for struggling readers, 134
VISION: shared, development of, 154–156
VISUAL DISPLAY STRATEGIES: for vocabulary instruction, 49–52
VOCABULARY, 3, 42–59; number of encounters/exposures to words, 48; number of words to teach, 46–47; selection of, 47
VOCABULARY INSTRUCTION: definition of, 44; effective, 48; questions on, 46–48; strategies for, 49–56; time frame for, 57
VOLUME: of reading, and struggling readers, 130–131

W–Y

WELFARE FAMILIES: oral language in, 91–92
WORD HUNT, 37
WRITING, 3–4, 106–115; teaching, 107–113
WRITING MARATHONS, 107–109
YIN/YANG, 10